Contents

Introduction

*V*ienna's rich historic legacy has made it a Mecca for tourists, who come in ever-increasing numbers to admire its baroque grandeur, to sample the atmosphere of its cafés and wine-taverns or to bask in the fabled glow of the 'golden Viennese heart'.

In the past, Vienna had other roles to play. Under the Romans it was a garrison town protecting the Danubian frontier line against the warlike Germanic tribes; the Babenbergs made it a glittering centre of culture and of east-west trade. Then came the Habsburgs, who turned it into an imperial capital and residence, at one moment the heart and brain of the largest empire ever ruled by a single monarch.

The Habsburgs

It is the Habsburgs who have left their imprint most visibly on the city; they were responsible for transforming St Stephen's into a magnificent Gothic cathedral and initiated the baroque churches such as St Peter's and St Charles Borromeo. Their greatest legacies, however, are their two splendid imperial residences: the Hofburg and Schloss Schönbrunn.

The Ringstrasse sweeps past Parlament

If the Habsburgs and the nobility of the baroque period are responsible for most of the Inner City's architectural splendours, the famous Ringstrasse that encircles it is the product of a new age and a newly powerful class. When Emperor Francis Joseph ordered the cincture of bastions and military exercise grounds to be demolished in 1857, the recently rich industrialists and entrepreneurs built themselves palatial residences all along the new thoroughfare. In between them rose the great symbolic public buildings associated with liberalism, the wealthy middle classes and democracy.

The Viennese

It is easy (but quite wrong) to dismiss the evident attachment of the Viennese to the past as blinkered conservatism. Some of the harshest criticism in this vein has traditionally come either from the sceptical Viennese themselves, or from intellectuals who settled here (especially at the turn of the century, when the Empire was in decline). The architect Adolf Loos wrote in favour of modernism and functionalism, in which he denounced 'ornament' on buildings as a 'crime'.

The Viennese are essentially survivors, as they like to stress in their proverbs and aphorisms: 'If you have an enemy, settle yourself on the threshold of your house and wait until his corpse is carried by.'

Some of these contradictions and conflicts may become apparent to visitors who decide to linger a week or two in Vienna. They will be impressed by the cleanliness of the city and the efficiency of its public transport, which includes a spotless Underground and almost noiseless trams, but then will be bombarded with details of the mega-scandals of the last two decades that have swallowed millions of Schillings of taxpayers' money. They will enjoy some theatrical or operatic performance, only to learn with astonishment that nobody has a good word to say for it. Leaving some eatery where the 'golden Viennese heart' would appear to have been invented, they will be arrested by the sight of motorists displaying unbridled aggression and *Schadenfreude*. As Gottfried Heindl put it: 'It is their inner contradictions that make the Viennese so 'difficult'. Almost everything one says about them is true; but usually its opposite is also not false.'

Looking across Vienna's rooftops by night – the splendour of the city's architecture illuminated

THOMAS COOK'S VIENNA

Vienna, although at its most magnificent in Thomas Cook's day, was not a popular destination for his tours; his clients preferred the scenic attractions of the Tyrol. However, in 1874 Cook organised and transported Queen Victoria's agricultural managers and their exhibit of prize cattle to the Vienna Agricultural Exhibition.

Cook's American clients seemed more interested in Vienna as a destination. For instance, a Grand Tour of Europe from the US arranged by Cook's in 1889 spent three days there, and the same was true in a similar tour arranged for US guests as late as 1924.

History

15BC–AD433
Vindobona is a Roman camp on the periphery of the empire.

976-1246
The Margraves of Babenberg rule Austria.

1155
Heinrich II of Babenberg sets up court in Vienna.

1246
The Babenberg line dies out.

1251–78
Ottokar of Bohemia rules in Austria.

1278
Rudolf I of Habsburg defeats Ottokar. 640 years of Habsburg rule begin.

1358
Rudolf IV lays the foundation stone for the south tower of St Stephen's.

1526
Ferdinand I inherits the thrones of Bohemia and Hungary.

1529
First Turkish siege of the city.

1551
Ferdinand I summons the Jesuits to Vienna. Counter-Reformation begins.

1679
One of the worst of many plague epidemics in the city.

1683
Jan Sobieski, King of Poland, and Archduke Karl rescue Vienna from the second great Turkish siege.

1740–80
Maria Theresa introduces many administrative, legal and educational reforms.

1781
The enlightened Joseph II issues his Edict of Tolerance for all faiths.

1805 and 1809
Napoleon occupies Vienna.

1806
Emperor Franz II renounces the title of Holy Roman Emperor having become the first 'Emperor of Austria' in 1804.

1814–15
The Congress of Vienna settles the political map after the Napoleonic wars.

1848
Revolution against Metternich's repressive system. Francis Joseph becomes emperor and rules until 1916.

1857
Francis Joseph orders the bastions of the city to be demolished. Beginning of the Ringstrasse era.

1867
The 'Compromise' with Hungary brings about the Austro-Hungarian Empire.

1918
Following defeat in World War I, the Empire collapses and a Republic is proclaimed in Austria.

1920-1934
The period of 'Red Vienna' when Social-Democratic rule in the city carries through an ambitious programme of housing and social welfare.

1934
Civil war in Vienna between the Social-Democratic faction and government forces.

1938
Hitler annexes Austria (the Anschluss).

Degraded to a province of Nazi Germany, the country participates in World War II.

1945

Occupation of Austria by the Russians, then the allies. Vienna is divided into four sectors.

1955

The Austrian State Treaty, signed in the Belvedere Palace, liberates the country. The Second Republic declares permanent neutrality.

VIENNA QUOTES

'There must be spectacles; a city needs that.'
Maria Theresa, (ruled 1740 to 1780).

'Vienna still belongs to Europe, but Asia begins on the Landstrasse [just east of the city centre]...'
Clemens Wenzel Lothar, Prince Metternich.

'I live in Vienna because I can only work in a village.'
Johannes Brahms, who lived in Vienna from 1862 until his death in 1897.

'A city that's easier to love and hate than to understand or leave.'
Hugo von Hofmannsthal.

Circular plan of Vienna

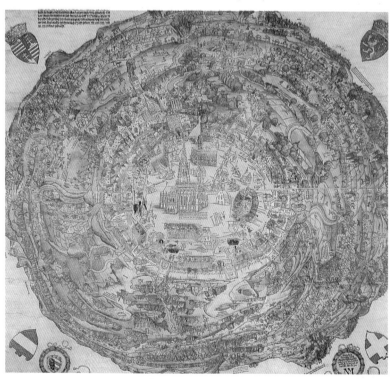

Political Vienna

On 1 January 1922, Vienna became one of the nine self-governing *Länder* (provinces) of the Austrian Republic, giving it a role that is quite distinct from its other one of *Bundeshauptstadt*, or capital of the country. The first fully democratic elections to the city council were held on 4 May 1919 and dislodged the right-wing Christian Social Party that had been in power since 1896 on a limited franchise. Since 1945 every freely elected Mayor of Vienna (who is also Governor of the Province) has been socialist.

New image

From 1920 to 1934, great strides were made in housing and social welfare, the money for which was raised by heavy taxation of the better off. Everywhere you can see the legacy of this – the huge blocks of social housing with the year of their erection displayed prominently on their façades, and the public facilities, such as the Amalienbad (swimming-baths) on Reumannplatz with a capacity for 1,300 people. The city planners and architects of the 1920s gave the traditionally conservative city a new image: functional, egalitarian, socially engaged.

'Red Vienna', however, was increasingly the target of the suspicions of the right wing and of the church, which were the dominant forces in all the other provinces of Austria. Tensions between the two camps exploded into civil war in 1934, followed by the imposition of a clerico-fascist dictatorship and the removal of Vienna's Socialist mayor. This in turn was followed by the Hitler regime. Only after World War II was a proper democratic city council reintroduced.

Tourism

The post-war Socialist administration has shrewdly exploited the financial benefits of increasing money flowing in from tourism and (until recently) a declining population. The cash has been used to maintain and improve the

Karl-Marx-Hof – part of Vienna's ambitious social housing scheme

Waiting to board a bus at Wein Station

Curtain in 1989 opened up the prospect of a further influx from the East into a city that is already host to the majority of Austria's *Gastarbeiter* (primarily Yugoslavs, but also Turks and Poles). Civil war in Yugoslavia has put pressure on the schools, as families have been brought to safety from the danger areas. Right-wing politicians have been quick to exploit the resultant social tensions.

The way ahead

Despite all this Vienna remains one of the safest, cleanest and best-run cities in the world. The challenges now facing its political élite are not exclusive to the city, nor worse than elsewhere: traffic congestion with its attendant pollution, an under-class of (sometimes) illegal immigrants exploited in the black economy, and unreal property prices are just some of them. With healthy cash flow and strong institutions of local government, Vienna may be better placed than most cities to deal with them.

infrastructure and give generous grants to cultural activities. There are, of course, problems. Unemployment has traditionally been higher and economic growth slower in the capital than elsewhere; while regions to the west appeared to be eager to get into the 21st century, Vienna with its ageing population and orientation to the past seemed (to its critics) to risk declining into a cross between a museum and an old people's home. Even the ambitious project of a joint 'world exhibition' with Budapest in 1995 foundered, among other things, on its decisive rejection by the Viennese in a referendum held in 1991.

In fact, this rejection seemed to demonstrate an awareness of the forces that threaten the heritage that is such a money spinner for the city. Tourist buses clog the traffic in the centre and the high-season flood of visitors is beginning to put a strain on the urban facilities and the patience of the inhabitants. Vienna is in danger of becoming a victim of its own success.

The problem of tourism is less sensitive, however, than that of the increasing number of immigrants, traditionally the object of Viennese mistrust. The sudden lifting of the Iron

Mozart out and about at the Opera

Culture

*T*he sharpest ever critic of Viennese society and culture was the satirist Karl Kraus (1874–1936). It was he who remarked that 'the streets of Vienna are surfaced with culture as the streets of other cities are with asphalt'. Kraus did not intend this entirely as a compliment, of course. Late 19th-century Vienna seemed to be intoxicated with aestheticism, eroticism, waltzes and operetta. Role-playing, display and factional criticism were the life-blood of a city filled with international artists.

A scene from Die Fledermaus

Musical heritage

Some of this tradition is alive and well today. Vienna is still a great centre for theatre, which offers everything from exclusively Viennese fare (Nestroy, Raimund, Grillparzer) to foreign or experimental work. The State Opera maintains its international reputation, and the Wiener Philharmonic remains one of the two or three really great orchestras of the world. Vienna's character and charm has been transmitted above all through its musical heritage: the mere mention of the city conjures up images of *The Magic Flute* with its happy ending and the delightfully unheroic character of Papageno; of the slightly melancholy eroticism of high society at the time of Maria Theresa in *Der Rosenkavalier*; the champagne sparkle of *Die Fledermaus*, or the flowing melody of a Schubert song, a Strauss waltz, a Mahler adagietto. 'Austria first found its soul in music and it is this that conquered the world', wrote the poet Hugo von Hofmannsthal. Today the soul of Vienna still throbs through its music.

Art and architecture

In recent years much attention has been paid internationally to Viennese painting at the turn of the century, and in particular to Gustav Klimt and the members of the Viennese Secession, as well as the Expressionists like Oskar

Multi-coloured Hundertwasserhaus

The arts

Theatre, literature and music suffered from 1938 with the loss of Jewish talent, and artistic creativity took some time to revive after the war. In the 1960s, however, things began to get lively in the art scene with the violent 'happenings' of 'Actionism', followed by the commercially successful school of 'Magical Realism'. In literature, few modern Austrian writers have made an impact in the English-speaking world, the best-known being Thomas Bernhard, whose dramas express a not untypical attitude of love-hatred towards his fatherland in general and Vienna in particular. In the same period cabaret and satire also had a new boom with Helmut Qualtinger's brilliant creation of 'Herr Karl', the epitome of Viennese *petit-bourgeois* turncoat opportunism.

Kokoschka and Egon Schiele. From the same period comes the Secessionist architecture of Otto Wagner, who built a number of celebrated public buildings (see pages 75 and 97) and designed the stations for the city railway. Going back in time from Wagner to the 'Ringstrasse era' (1857–1890), there are monumental buildings in various historical styles on or around the Ring. In the old Inner City are the baroque palaces and churches of Fischer von Erlach, Lukas von Hildebrandt and others, not to mention the great Gothic churches such as St Stephen's and Maria am Gestade. Modern additions to this rich legacy of architecture are comparatively few, but the multi-coloured dwelling house designed by the artist Friedensreich Hundertwasser (1985) has become a tourist attraction, as has also Hans Hollein's elegant Haas Haus (1990) opposite the cathedral.

Severely modern Haas Haus

Vienna has always had a massive amount to offer in terms of musical or theatrical productions, and of exhibitions and museums overflowing with treasures collected by the Habsburgs, not to mention the more informal pleasures of the tavern, the cabaret or the wine cellar. If Dr Johnson had visited the city, he would certainly have opined that 'a man who is tired of Vienna is tired of life'.

Geography

*L*ooking back on Viennese history, the writer Ferdinand Kürnberger attributed the city's rise to greatness largely to geographical factors despite its peripheral position in northern Austria. The position of Vienna he described as: '(lying) where the foothills of the Norican Alps give way to the Pannonian plain, on the intersection of the diagonals which can be drawn from Poland and Russia to Italy, and from Germany to Byzantium. (The city stands) at the very point of the Danube that lies closest to the sources of the Elbe and the Oder, and almost at exactly the same distance from Germans, Italians and the Slavs of the Northern or Southern Groups. (This position) predestined it to become a capital'.

View across Vienna's rooftops to the graceful spire of Stephansdom

Past importance

In the Middle Ages the three great cities of central Europe were Cracow, Vienna and Prague (it is often forgotten that Vienna is actually east of Prague). While the other two declined, Vienna retained its pre-eminence, not least because of its status as capital of the Habsburgs' central European empire. Its importance as a market, trading centre and political focal point meant also that it was always cosmopolitan. Some of the street names in the old town recall the foreigners who did business in Vienna in the Middle Ages and their trades (for example,

Tuchlauben, where the Flemish cloth merchants sold their wares). Judenplatz and Judengasse recall the Jewish ghetto that was dissolved with the first pogrom against the Jews in 1421. Although they gradually returned, they were expelled again in 1670. The 19th and early 20th century saw a massive Jewish influx from Russia, Poland and Galicia, so that in 1938 the population that fell victim to the Nazis numbered around 200,000. The same period saw thousands of Slavs and other nationalities of the empire settling in the capital.

The Danube

In all this coming and going and commercial activity the Danube played a crucial role. Until its regulation in the 1870s however, the Viennese attitude to it was by no means so enthusiastic as Strauss's untruthfully titled waltz, *On the Beautiful Blue Danube*, would suggest. In the past, flooding was frequent, it was never blue, and around Vienna not really beautiful either. The best view of it can be had from the Leopoldsberg, including the artificially constructed Danube Canal (1875), that washes the walls of the Inner City, and the 21km–long riverbed of the 'New Danube' dug out only in the 1970s. The latter works created the long thin Danube Island (see page 128) as a summer playground for the inhabitants.

Although Vienna was never a city on the Danube in the sense that Paris is on the Seine, its microclimate has always been influenced by the great river. The Vienna woods and the now increasingly dried out meadows and swamps (including the Prater) are part of its legacy. The south-facing hills along its banks are carpeted with vineyards that flourish due to its benign effects.

The far from 'blue' Danube

Climatic factors

In addition to the influence of the Danube, Vienna is subjected to various contrasting climatic forces because of its geographical situation – damper maritime winds come from the west, while the south and east are characterised by the more extreme temperatures of the great Pannonian plain. The Alpine barrier often produces a particular local effect of strong, warmish winds from the southwest (the so-called *Föhn*), which can be unpleasant for those with circulation problems. All these factors mean that you can experience remarkable differences in the microclimate depending upon whether you live close to the Danube in Vienna, or far from it on a hillside, or in the *Wiener Becken* to the west or to the south and southeast. Many feel that the Viennese character is similarly multi-faceted. As the writer György Sebestyén put it: 'The indolent and rather barbarous way of life of the German South is here irradiated by the influence of Mediterranean culture and given strength by the archaic forces of South-Eastern Europe.'

Finding your feet

When to come

Central Europe usually enjoys a long Indian Summer from early in September to mid- or sometimes late October. At this time the balmy weather is ideal for sight-seeing: in the city or the wine villages you can still sit outside until early evening; around Vienna, the neighbouring countryside and the Danube valley is filled with autumnal radiance. The natural consequence is that hoteliers regard the autumn as high season and charge accordingly. It may also be difficult to get a hotel room unless you book well in advance, although a package tour makes things easier.

Younger people may be more inclined to brave the (often ferocious) mid-summer heat and there is plenty of mass tourism, too, between June and August. Spring seems to emerge overnight from a usually bitter winter. Warm clothes are still required in March and April against the ever-chilling winds.

Village on the Kahlenberg hill

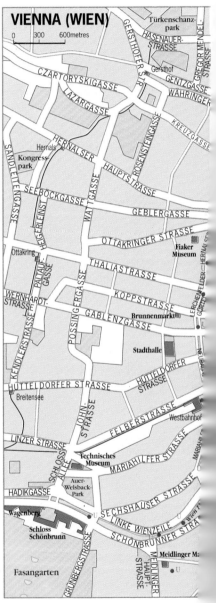

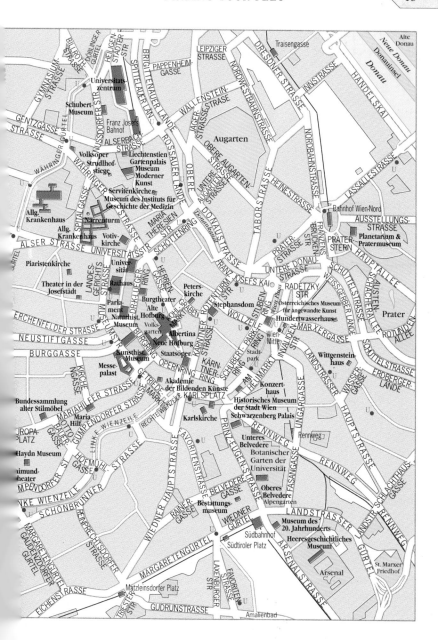

Arrival and Departure

Vienna has an international airport at Schwechat, 19km southeast of the city, with all modern facilities and good transfer connections to the city (see **Practical Guide**). The once great Austro-Hungarian Empire has left a legacy of vast railway stations, now again coming into their own since the fall of the Iron Curtain. The Westbahnhof serves Western Europe, including Hungary and Romania; the Südbahnhof serves Italy and Yugoslavia, and also Hungary, Poland and Czechoslovakia; while the recently reconstructed Franz-Josefs-Bahnhof has good connections to Berlin and Prague. Since the orientation of each station does not necessarily correspond to the destination of its trains, all tickets need to be carefully checked for point of departure.

Vienna is approached by a West Motorway and a Southern one. The East Motorway continues beyond the airport and will soon reach the Hungarian border. A ring-road links these three routes.

Driving in Vienna

The Inner City, Vienna's oldest part, is encircled by a Ringstrasse built in the second half of the 19th century. Within the Ring parking has become a nightmare, although there are several underground car parks (see **Practical Guide**). Short-term parking slots are marked with a blue line (tickets and cardboard clocks are available from tobacconists known as *Trafik*).

Apart from the difficulties of parking, the motorist faces the additional hazard of a labyrinth of one-way streets in and beyond the Ring, which threatens to carry unversed drivers far out of their way. There are also trams to contend with, sometimes (as on the Ring itself) coming against you on a one-way street. Tram stops require care, especially where there is no raised platform on the road, for then the driver is obliged to let passengers descend and ascend in front before proceeding.

All these factors (together with the unrestrained aggression of some Viennese drivers) may persuade many motorists to leave their vehicles in a car park or garage and use public transport whenever possible.

Getting around

The inner city is sufficiently compact to be covered on foot – and indeed its core along the Kohlmarkt, the Graben and Kärntner Strasse is actually a pedestrian zone. If you get footsore, there are hopper buses operating between Schwarzenbergplatz or Dr-Karl-Renner-Ring and Schwedenplatz (3A and 2A), which cover its nodal points. The U-Bahn (underground – U1 and the newly constructed U3) also traverse part of it. On the Ring and beyond it are trams and buses, as well as the network of five U-Bahn lines and suburban railway connections. The most economic solution to getting about is to buy a season ticket which entitles you to travel on all means of public transport over a wide area, alone or in groups, and which is available for different periods of time or, undated, for a number of complete days (see **Practical Guide**). Vienna does not go to sleep as early as it used to, but public transport (except for a few 'night-bus' routes which depart from Schwedenplatz 2) generally ceases around midnight.

Manners and mores

The Viennese may seem to be a mass of

The impressive Burgtheater: a traditional German-speaking theatre

contradictions - worldly but provincial, cynical yet sentimental, good-natured and helpful yet sometimes aggressively ill-natured and obstructive. This has something to do with the weather perhaps, but certainly a lot to do with their history. When the Habsburg court represented the fount of all pecuniary or social advancement, the shrewd man learned to bow and scrape convincingly before his patrons. By the same token, intrigue, backbiting and slanderous gossip thrived in a world where favours were fiercely competed for.

A different side of the Viennese, the more homely one, comes out in their fondness for simple but sensual pleasure; lingering in one of the many coffee-houses or going with friends to the *Heurigen* (wine-tavern) and ending the evening with a rendering of a sentimental Viennese song. Such pleasures come under the general heading of *gemütlich*, a word which covers a spectrum of perceptions associated with Vienna, including geniality, cosiness, and comfort.

THE COST OF LIVING

It is no good pretending that Vienna is a particularly cheap city. High rates of VAT and local taxes and high duties on imported goods have ensured in the past that prices remained rather high. That is beginning to change however: Austria's application to join the European Community (and its entry meanwhile into the European Economic Area agreement) has necessitated some revision of traditional habits and liberalisation of duties. In any case, the relentless rise in the cost of living in some neighbouring countries, notably Italy, now places Vienna in a more favourable light.

Vienna State Opera House, Staatsoper

Some items remain relatively good value or are downright cheap. The cheapest (standing) tickets for the Staatsoper compare favourably with prices charged at other opera houses of world status and offer unrestricted vision of the stage; those for the Volksoper are decidedly economic, since one is not paying for international stars, but nevertheless getting first-rate performances. Food, though of a high quality, is generally expensive, but provided you stick to the house wine, drink will be one of the cheaper items on

Café Central: enjoyable, but not cheap

your bill in a restaurant. Meals in the traditional hostelries – *Weinkeller, Bierstuben, Beisls* - are fairly priced by European standards. The new self-service chains (*Naschmarkt, Nordsee*) are even better value. (See **Food and Drink.**)

On the other hand the hard-to-resist pastries and cakes of the *Konditorei* (patisserie) and a simple cup of coffee will prove to be relatively expensive. In the former case you are paying for a luxury and in the latter you are incidentally purchasing the privilege to sit in the coffee-house all day, if you so desire. Accommodation and public transport are also quite costly, as are books, on which VAT is levied.

Viennese dialect

'Viennese dialect' writes Gottfried Heindl 'does not fulfil the traditional function of speech of making oneself understood, but the opposite one of erecting a barrier (against the outside world).' If this is discouraging, it is some consolation to discover that even

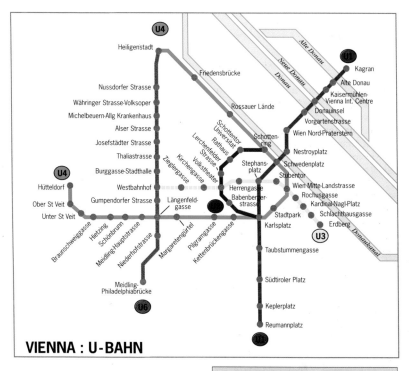

VIENNA : U-BAHN

Germans can be at a loss when confronted with the rapid-fire consonant-squelching speech of the born Viennese.

Some dialect words or expressions have acquired an almost emblematic function to describe local characteristics – for example the word *Schmäh*, which conjures visions of 'getting away with it' (blarney), and *raunzen*, which means to grumble.

Even the *Hochdeutsch* (standard language) that some may have learned in school has picturesque variants in local usage for many everyday items. Preservation of these forms is one way the Austrians try to resist the cultural imperialism of their German cousins.

COMING TO TERMS WITH THE VIENNESE
'The municipal vice of Vienna is a sort of laziness, an easy-going spirit which quickly degenerates into slackness. The quality is recognised by the Viennese, who are not hypocrites, and called by them *Schlamperei*. It is shared by the highest and the lowest, causing the former to lose battles, the latter to forget errands...'
EDWARD CRANKSHAW

'The Austrians are as German as the Danube is blue...'
ALFRED POLGAR

Areas of Vienna

*T*he *Stadt Wien*, which is a city and a province, has seen most of its expansion from the original historic core in the last 150 years. Vienna now contains 23 *Bezirke*, or urban districts, which are grouped in two concentric circles round the First District (the *Innere Stadt*, or Inner City). The compact Districts 2 to 9 huddle round old Vienna, while Districts 10 to 23 sprawl outwards in varying shapes and sizes.

Vienna's colourful and varied architecture

The Districts of Vienna

1   Innere Stadt (the historic Inner City)
2   Leopoldstadt (named after the Emperor Leopold I, following his expulsion of the Jews from this area)
3   Landstrasse (centred on a road that goes back to Roman times)
4   Wieden (the name is a corruption from 'Viennese suburb on the River Wien')
5   Margareten (apparently named after Margaret of Tyrol, wife of Rudolf IV)
6   Mariahilf (a copy of a famous icon of the Madonna – the Mariahilf – is lodged in a church here)
7   Neubau (literally 'New Building': the name dates to 1693)
8   Josefstadt (after the Emperor Joseph I, 1678–1711)
9   Alsergrund (after the Als stream that once flowed here)
10 Favoriten (after the imperial Favorita palace)
11 Simmering
12 Meidling
13 Hietzing
14 Penzing
15 Rudolfsheim-Fünfhaus
16 Ottakring
17 Hernals
18 Währing
19 Döbling
20 Brigittenau
21 Floridsdorf (north of the Danube)
22 Donaustadt (north of the Danube)
23 Liesing

Vienna has two asphalt corsets: the Ringstrasse round the Inner City and the *Gürtel* or 'Belt' that operates as a south-circular road through the suburbs. It runs from the Danube below Heiligenstadt in the west to the Landstrasse area in the east. Beyond the *Gürtel* the city degenerates into subtopia with factories and hypermarkets in the south and southeast, while in the north and southwest it merges into the attractive wine-villages on the slopes of

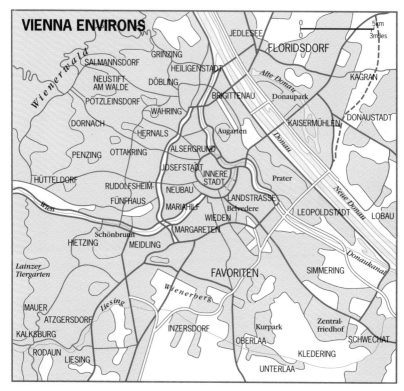

VIENNA ENVIRONS

JEDLESEE · FLORIDSDORF · KAGRAN · DONAUSTADT · Alte Donau · Donaupark · KAISERMÜHLEN · Donau · Neue Donau · LOBAU · Donaukanal · GRINZING · HEILIGENSTADT · SALMANNSDORF · NEUSTIFT AM WALDE · DÖBLING · BRIGITTENAU · Wienerwald · PÖTZLEINSDORF · WÄHRING · Augarten · DORNACH · HERNALS · ALSERGRUND · PENZING · OTTAKRING · JOSEFSTADT · INNERE STADT · Prater · HÜTTELDORF · RUDOLFSHEIM · NEUBAU · Wien · FÜNFHAUS · MARIAHILF · LANDSTRASSE · Belvedere · LEOPOLDSTADT · WIEDEN · Schönbrunn · MARGARETEN · HIETZING · MEIDLING · Lainzer Tiergarten · FAVORITEN · SIMMERING · MAUER · Wienerberg · ATZGERSDORF · Liesing · KALKSBURG · INZERSDORF · Kurpark · Zentral-friedhof · SCHWECHAT · RODAUN · LIESING · OBERLAA · KLEDERING · UNTERLAA

0 5 km
0 3 miles

the Wienerwald (Viennese Woods). North of the Danube are situated the traditionally poorer areas, together with green spaces such as the Augarten and the Prater.

The Donaustadt (22nd District) contains the so-called UNO-City, constructed between 1973 and 1976, which houses organs of the United Nations and some spectacular new conference centres.

Tourists are likely to spend most of their time in the old city (First District), where the baroque palaces, the churches and the Hofburg are concentrated. This Innere Stadt is delineated by the Ringstrasse which follows the old city walls.

Adjoining it are the Third and Fourth Districts (Landstrasse and Wieden), the former containing the diplomatic quarter and the Belvedere Palace, the latter the great Karlskirche. Favoriten has been a working class district since the influx of Czech construction workers in the 19th century, while, at the other end of the scale, Hietzing (which adjoins Schönbrunn) boasts a café (Dommayer) where Johann Strauss Jr entertained the families of the imperial officials and the prosperous bourgeoisie; the latter remain its typical residents.

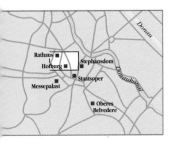

From Ringstrasse to the Romans

This walk combines some of the finest buildings of the Ringstrasse era (from 1857 to 1890) with baroque palaces and Gothic churches. *Allow 1 hour*

Begin from the inner side of the Ringstrasse at the tram stop (1) for Dr-Karl-Renner-Ring. Walk northwards and enter the Volksgarten on your right at the entrance opposite the Parlament (Parliament) across the Ring.

Nearby:

Parlament (opposite

entrance to

Volksgarten)

·Rathaus (opposite the

Burgtheater)

1 VOLKSGARTEN

The 'people's garden' was laid out in 1823 by Peter von Nobile and contains his imitation of the Theseion in Athens, now used for exhibitions of modern art. Among the ornaments are Anton Fernkorn's picturesque fountain with dolphins and the monument to Empress Elisabeth (Kaiserin-Elisabeth Denkmal), who was murdered in 1898 by an anarchist (see pages 117 and 122).
Leave by the gate at the northern end. In front of you is the Burgtheater.

2 BURGTHEATER

The Burgtheater was erected in 1888 to replace a smaller

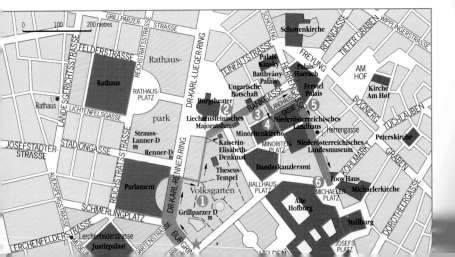

baroque one on Michaelerplatz which had been attached to the Hofburg. The stairs have frescos by Gustav and Ernst Klimt and Franz Matsch (tours of the interior daily), and include a representation of Shakespeare's Globe Theatre (see pages 53 and 147).

Behind the Burgtheater walk down Bankgasse.

3 BANKGASSE

Immediately on your right at no 9 is the Liechtensteinisches Majoratshaus, the Viennese residence of the tiny principality's rulers, designed by Domenico Martinelli and others. At nos 4 to 6 is the Ungarische Botschaft (Hungarian Embassy), which consists of two family palaces knocked together between 1783 and 1784 by Franz Hillebrand; beyond it is the Batthyány-Palais (see page 90) where the beautiful Hungarian Countess, Eleonore Batthyány, used to play whist with her aged admirer, Prince Eugene of Savoy. It is said that he stayed so long the coachman was usually asleep when he left, but the carriage horses knew the way home to the Belvedere Palais on their own.

Halfway along Bankgasse turn to the right into Minoritenplatz.

4 MINORITENKIRCHE

Flanked on three sides by magnificent baroque and neo-classical façades is the plain Gothic church of the Minorite order. Its oldest part dates to the late 14th century, since when it has suffered many changes of fortune, including having the top of its steeple knocked off in the Turkish siege of 1683. After King Ottokar of Bohemia was defeated on the Marchfeld, northeast of Vienna, by Rudolf of Habsburg in 1278, his body was put on public view in this church. That defeat marked the beginning of 640 years of Habsburg rule in Austria. Rudolf himself was accepted into the Minorite order after the battle (see page 60).

Leave Minoritenplatz by Landhausgasse, then turn right along Herrengasse.

5 HERRENGASSE

The street of the Herren or 'lords' is so named after the aristocracy who used to own palaces here (dating from the 16th to the early 19th century), conveniently close to the Hofburg and the court. At no 13 is the Niederösterreichisches Landhaus (Diet of the province of Lower Austria), the dramatic proceedings of which in 1848 were the prelude to the revolution of that year.

Head south towards Michaelerplatz.

6 MICHAELERPLATZ

The ancient Roman road met the exit from the camp of *Vindobona* in this square, and excavations in the centre have recently revealed Roman brothels, as well as later baroque structures. On the right is the entrance to the Alte Hofburg, on the east side the Gothic Michaelerkirche (St Michael's Church – see page 59) and on the corner with the Kohlmarkt the controversial house designed by Adolf Loos. The Emperor Francis Joseph so disliked the building he ordered that the curtains of the Hofburg rooms directly opposite it should be kept permanently drawn, lest he should pass by and accidentally glance out of the window at it (see page 115).

From Michaelerplatz, hopper bus 2A takes you back to Dr-Karl-Renner-Ring, or walk there through the courtyards of the Hofburg and the Heldenplatz.

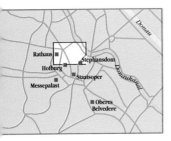

The Ancient Core of the City

This is a longer walk that takes you through some of the oldest areas of the city, albeit often overlaid with much later buildings. *Allow about 1 hour 40 minutes*

Nearby

Mölker Bastei

Pasqualatihaus

Salvatorkapelle

Schottenkirche

Start from the major tram junction at Schottentor. Emerge from the underpass at the beginning of Schottengasse and walk to Freyung.

1 FREYUNG

The name of this irregularly shaped square goes back to the right of asylum once granted to miscreants who escaped into the monastery of the Irish monks on the north side of it. On the west side is the graceful façade of the Palais-Kinsky (no 4) designed by Lukas von Hildebrandt (1716). To the south is the vast Palais-Harrach (no 3) belonging to a noble family on whose estates Haydn was born. Adjoining it is the so-called Ferstel Palais, named after the architect, with the famous Café Central (see page 62). An elegant shopping arcade runs through the complex, which once housed the stock exchange. *Walk southwards through a part known as Heidenschuss, after the ornament on the wall of a Turk on horseback brandishing a scimitar.*

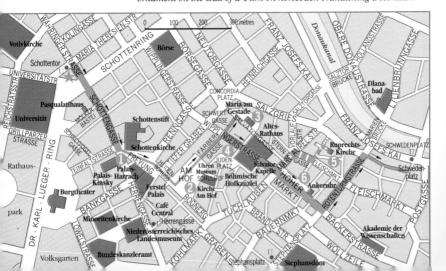

2 AM HOF

On the site of what is now the Kirche
Am Hof (Church of the Nine Choirs of
Angels) the Babenberg Duke Heinrich II
set up his court in the 12th century, thus
making Vienna a capital city for the first
time (see page 58). When he built a new
palace close to what is now the Hofburg,
the mint was put here instead. Later the
Carmelites erected a monastery and
church on the same site. Alongside the
church runs the Schulhof with the
diminutive Obizzi Palais, containing the
Uhrenmuseum (clock museum). In the
southwest corner is the baroque façade
of the Bürgerliches Zeughaus (former
Citizens' Armoury – see page 53).
*Follow Färbergasse and Schwertgasse
northeast.*

3 MARIA AM GESTADE

'Maria on the river bank' (the Danube
once lapped at the bottom) is one of the
loveliest Gothic churches of Vienna.
Michael Knab built it in the early 15th
century (see page 59).
*Retrace your steps to the junction with
Wipplingerstrasse.*

4 WIPPLINGERSTRASSE

Walking east on this street you reach the
former Böhmische Hofkanzlei
(Bohemian Chancellery – see page 52) at
no 7, designed by Fischer von Erlach,
one of the greatest architects of the
baroque period. Its façade looks on to
Judenplatz, site of the medieval Jewish
ghetto that was razed to the ground in
the pogrom of 1421. At no 8 is the Altes
Rathaus (Old City Hall) – the last
meeting of the city council here was in
1885 before it moved to the building on
the Ringstrasse (see page 43).
*A detour to the left from Wipplingerstrasse
along Marc Aurel-Strasse passes*
*Salvatorgasse to the left and brings you to
Ruprechtsplatz on the right.*

5 RUPRECHTSKIRCHE

The plain church of St Rupert is the
oldest still standing in the old City. It is
named after the patron saint of salt
miners. The earliest churches in Vienna
were under the patronage of the
Salzburg Diocese, which was in vigorous
competition with that of Passau (see
page 61).
*Retrace your steps along Marc Aurel-Strasse
to the junction with Wipplingerstrasse and
turn left.*

The former Citizens' Armoury, Am Hof

6 HOHER MARKT

On the northwest corner the rulers of
Vienna during the Dark Ages probably
had their rudimentary 'palace'. On the
opposite side of the square, Roman
houses with a central heating system can
be visited below ground. At the
northeast end is the famous Ankeruhr
(Anker Clock), forming a bridge
between the two buildings of the 'Anker'
(Anchor) Insurance Company. At noon
figures from Austrian history parade
across the clock-face (see page 45).
*Turn left out of the Hoher Markt into
Rotenturmstrasse, which leads to the tram
junction of Schwedenplatz. The walk takes
you along the eastern periphery of the
original Roman Camp.*

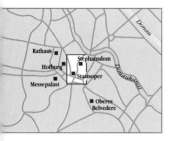

Modern Opulence and Imperial Echoes

This route takes in some of the noblest buildings and most fashionable areas of Vienna. *Allow 1 hour*

Nearby

Neuer Markt

Donner Brunnen

Kapuzinerkirche

Begin by the Staatsoper (Opera House) which stands close to the tram and U-Bahn junction of Karlsplatz/Oper.

1 ALBERTINAPLATZ

The square adjoins the Opera House and Hotel Sacher (on the eastern edge) which itself was next to Café Mozart (now a shop), where scenes from the Carol Reed film classic, *The Third Man*, were shot. The square takes its name from the famous collection of prints and drawings on the south side, the basis of which was gathered by Duke Albert of Sachsen-Teschen, the husband of Maria Theresa's daughter, Marie Christine. In the middle is a modern memorial by Alfred Hrdlicka recalling the evils of war and Fascism. On the north side is the lovely Lobkowitz-Palais (Lobkowitzplatz 2) by Fischer von Erlach, where Beethoven gave a private première of the *Eroica Symphony* in 1804 (see page 42).

2 AUGUSTINERKIRCHE

Adjoining the Albertina to the west is the severe Gothic Augustinerkirche (Church of the Augustines), which offers a rich programme of sung masses on Sundays. The tomb of the previously mentioned Marie Christine by Antonio Canova (1805) is spectacular. The hearts of the Habsburg rulers are kept in silver urns here (see page 56).

Proceed along Augustinerstrasse to Josefsplatz.

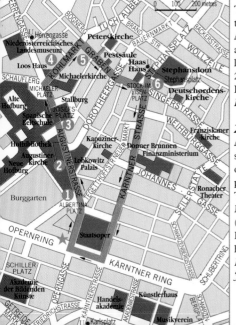

3 JOSEFSPLATZ

The square is named after Emperor Joseph II, an equestrian statue of whom stands in the centre. It is dominated by the baroque architecture of the two Fischer von Erlachs, father and son. To the south is the Hofbibliothek (Court Library) with a magnificent marbled and wood interior and a cupola fresco by Daniel Gran. The buildings are joined by east and west wings, the latter affording entry to the Spanische Reitschule, where 'morning training' of the Lippizaners may be watched. This is also where performances take place. The interior was designed by the younger Fischer von Erlach. Across the street from it is the Stallburg, a rare Renaissance survival in Vienna.

Continue north into Michaelerplatz and turn right.

Elegant shopping in the Kohlmarkt

4 KOHLMARKT

The name of this now fashionable shopping street comes from charcoal, which was once sold here. Haydn lived in a garret of the house immediately on the right and got his first big break when he met Metastasio, the court librettist, who lived in grander rooms on a lower floor. At no 14 is Demel's Konditorei, famous for its exotic pastries, elegant interior and appalling acoustics.

At the end of the Kohlmarkt turn right.

Sightseeing Graben by fiaker

5 GRABEN

Originally this was the southern ditch protecting the Roman camp at *Vindobona* (see page 63). It is now the fashionable heart of Vienna, although until the turn of the century it was thronged with prostitutes known as 'Graben nymphs'. In the centre is the Plague Monument (see page 97), a dramatic baroque work partly designed by Fischer von Erlach. Emperor Leopold I (who is represented on it, kneeling in prayer) commissioned the work when the 1679 plague receded. Just off the Graben to the north is the great Peterskirche (Church of St Peter – see page 60), designed by Lukas von Hildebrandt.

Walk to the east end of Graben.

6 STOCK-IM-EISEN-PLATZ

This area to the southwest of the great Stephansdom (St Stephen's Cathedral – see Walk 4) is so called because of the nail-studded tree-trunk here. According to an old tradition, visiting locksmiths' apprentices knocked a nail into the stump. On the opposite side of the space is the newly erected Haas Haus by Hans Hollein (see page 63).

Turn right along the celebrated shopping mall of the Kärntner Strasse, which brings you back to the opera.

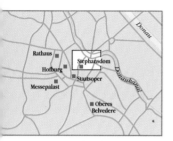

To the Glory of God...

This walk takes in a representative sample of Vienna's churches, beginning with the city's symbolic heart - Stephansdom (St Stephen's Cathedral). *Allow 2 hours*

1 STEPHANSDOM

Nearby

Synagogue,

Seitenstettengasse

Kornhäusel-Turm

The most interesting external features of St Stephen's are the Romanesque parts around and above the great west door, and the fabulous Gothic south tower, known to the locals as the 'Steffl'. Inside are Anton Pilgram's pulpit (1500), containing his famous self-portrait, and an enormous Renaissance tomb for the Emperor Frederick III (see pages 110-13 and 115). The cathedral was built over two centuries and became one of the focal points of the alliance between throne and altar in Catholic Austria, but more especially the citizens' own church. *Walk down Rotenturmstrasse from St Stephen's and turn right into Fleischmarkt.*

2 FLEISCHMARKT

At no 11 is the Griechenbeisl, a restaurant occupying a medieval building and the site of the earliest recorded inn of the city. The bagpiper Augustin, who survived a night lying

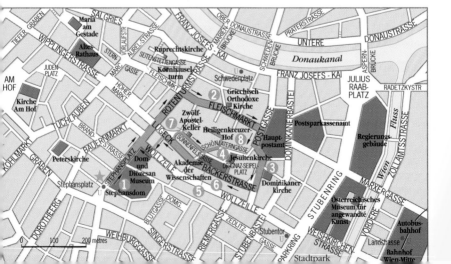

drunkenly on the corpses of plague victims after falling into the burial pit on his way home, was said to have been a regular. At no 15 is the richly glittering Griechisch-Orthodoxe Kirche (Greek Orthodox Church) designed by Theophil von Hansen in 1858 (see page 57).
At the end of the Fleischmarkt bear right into the Postgasse.

3 DOMINIKANERKIRCHE
At no 4 is the Dominican Church with an impressive baroque interior. The Dominicans were the ideological policemen of Catholicism, but never as influential in Vienna as the Jesuits (see page 57).
Turn right into Bäckerstrasse and shortly on the right is Dr-Ignaz-Seipel-Platz.

4 JESUITENKIRCHE
This striking Jesuit Church stands next to the Alte Universität (Old University – see page 43) along the east side of the square. The Jesuits were called to Vienna in 1551 by Ferdinand I. In 1623 they were given control of the University by Ferdinand II and allowed to build this church. It has a fine interior remodelled by Andrea Pozzo in 1705 (see page 58).

5 AKADEMIE DER WISSENSCHAFTEN
The west side of the square is occupied by the beautifully proportioned Akademie der Wissenschaften (Academy of Sciences, 1755). Not long after Jadot de Ville-Issey's building was completed, Canaletto did a painting of it (1761) which can be seen in the Kunsthistorisches Museum (Museum of Fine Arts). At that time it was the University's Faculty of Law, and had an

astronomical observatory on top. Since 1857 it has had its present function (see page 42).
Continue west into Bäckerstrasse.

6 BÄCKERSTRASSE
Originally Sonnenfelsgasse (parallel to the north) and Bäckerstrasse were the same street, or rather, a long narrow square. In the 16th century, pressure on space in the Innere Stadt (Inner City) necessitated building a row of houses along the middle of it. Behind 18th-century or later façades, some early patrician houses have been preserved. There are a number of splendid portals and a fine Renaissance courtyard behind the frontage of no 7.

7 ZWÖLF-APOSTEL-KELLER
At the end of Bäckerstrasse both it and the parallel Sonnenfelsgasse run into Lugeck. At no 3 Sonnenfelsgasse is an historic wine cellar going down three levels, the bottom level being medieval with baroque vaults above it.
Walk down Sonnenfelsgasse and turn left into Schönlaterngasse.

8 HEILIGENKREUZER HOF
At Schönlaterngasse no 5 a gateway gives access to the tranquil oasis of the Heiligenkreuzer Hof (see page 63). The oldest part of these city possessions of the Cistercian monastery at Heiligenkreuz (Holy Cross, see page 137) dates to Babenberg times (1170). It was given its present pleasing aspect in the 17th and 18th centuries with baroque façades and a chapel with a portal by Giovanni Giuliani (1729).
Retrace your steps to Lugeck and go through an alley to the Wollzeile. Turn right to Rotenturmstrasse.

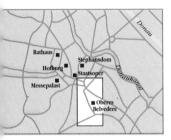

Earthly Powers

The walk encompasses proletarian propaganda and princely pomp. *Allow 1 hour (2 hours if Arsenal is included)*

Start at Schwarzenbergplatz

Nearby

Gardekirche (Polish National Church)

Salesianerinnenkirche (Church of the Salesians)

1 SCHWARZENBERGPLATZ

The large oblong square has lost its original function as gracious frontage to the family palace, but the statue (by Julius Hähnel) of Karl Philipp, Prince Schwarzenberg, on his horse still dominates the middle of it. He was the hero of the so-called Battle of the Nations against Napoleon in 1813, but the family produced many leading figures in Austrian history. An earlier Schwarzenberg had earned the gratitude of the Viennese by organising relief in a plague epidemic, when the other nobles fled. The current prince is head of the Czech chancellery and adviser to President Václav Havel (see page 93).

2 RUSSISCHES BEFREIUNGSDENKMAL

At the southern end of the square is a vast monument (Russian Liberation Monument) showing a Russian soldier carrying a flag and urging his comrades into action. It was the practice of the Red Army to rush up such bombastic monuments in the cities they 'liberated' in 1945. In front of it is the Hochstrahlbrunnen (High Spurting Fountain), around the basin of which are 365 little springs representing the days of the year; others symbolise the days of the week, months, hours of the day, etc. The fountain has provided pure drinking water since 1873.

From Schwarzenbergplatz take the Rennweg, as far as the Unteres Belvedere on your right at no 6.

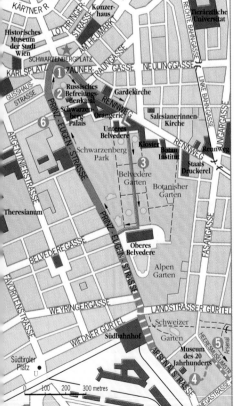

3 BELVEDERE

This great palace is divided into an upper representational part and a lower functional one, with a magnificent baroque garden in between. It was built for Prince Eugene of Savoy in the early 18th century. The latter had amassed an enormous fortune, partly through booty, but principally from the gifts a grateful emperor showered upon him for his generalship in the Turkish wars and against the French. The Unteres (Lower) Belvedere contains the Gothic and baroque museums and the Oberes (Upper) Belvedere houses Austrian painting and sculpture from the 19th century on (see pages 48–51).

Leave the Belvedere behind the upper palace, turning left into Prinz-Eugen-Strasse if the Museum des 20 Jahrhunderts (Museum of the 20th Century) and the Arsenal are included in the walk, right if not.

4 MUSEUM DES 20 JAHRHUNDERTS

The other side of the busy 'Gürtel' traffic artery is the Schweizer Garten in which the Museum of the 20th Century is situated. The building is based on the Austrian pavilion for the Brussels World Exhibition in 1958 and shows modern art (see page 78).

Take the Heeresmuseumstrasse through the park to the huge complex of the Arsenal.

5 HEERESGESCHICHTLICHES MUSEUM - ARSENAL

This enormous complex of buildings (74 in all) was built in the style of romantic historicism by Theophil von Hansen and others in 1854. The idea was to construct several formidable military barracks around the periphery of Vienna to prevent a repetition of the happenings of the 1848 Revolution. At that time citizens broke into the Armoury Am Hof (see page 25) and quickly provided themselves with weapons. The Heeresgeschichtliches Museum (Museum of Military History) is worth visiting for its splendid interior alone, with a Hall of Generals containing 56 statues and the Hall of Fame with frescos by Carl Blaas. A special room is dedicated to the murder of the Archduke Franz Ferdinand at Sarajevo, the spark that led to the conflagration of the First World War (see page 45).

From the Arsenal, return the way you came and descend Prinz-Eugen-Strasse back to Schwarzenbergplatz.

The formidable façade of the Arsenal

6 PALAIS SCHWARZENBERG

Palais Schwarzenberg was completed by Fischer von Erlach, a great rival of the Belvedere's architect, Hildebrandt. It was restored after being bombed in the war and is now one of the most prestigious hotels in Vienna, although the prince still occupies part of it.

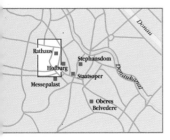

The Josefstadt and more...

Although bounded by two traffic arteries, Josefstadt retains the atmosphere and charm of a baroque 'suburb'. *Allow 1 hour*

Nearby

Spittelberg

Rathaus

Begin from the Volkstheater, where there is a U-Bahn station (U2/U6) and a tram stop (no 49).

1 VOLKSTHEATER

The 'German People's Theatre' was built in 1889 by the architects Ferdinand Fellner and Hermann Helmer. After various disastrous fires in the older theatres, it was decreed that it should be free-standing on all sides. Both technically and architecturally this was to become a model for theatres all over the vast realms of the Austro-Hungarian Empire, where near-replicas of it are often to be found, built by the same firm.

Walk behind the Volkstheater into a small park, overlooked on the south side by a baroque palace.

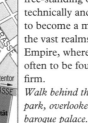

2 PALAIS-TRAUTSON

This fine palace (1712) was built by Johann Bernhard Fischer von Erlach for Prince Trautson, Chief Equerry to Emperor Joseph I. It came into the possession of Maria Theresa when the family died out, and was for a long time the headquarters of her exotically dressed Hungarian Lifeguards.

On the opposite side of busy Museumsstrasse is the new building of the vast Justizpalast (Palace of Justice); the former one was set on fire by demonstrating workers in 1927 after a politically motivated

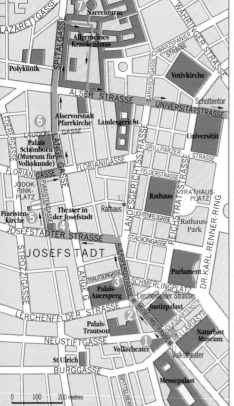

0 100 200 metres

miscarriage of justice.
*Continue north across the junction with
Lerchenfelder Strasse and Auerspergstrasse.*

3 PALAIS AUERSPERG

At no 1 Auerspergstrasse is a palace
originally designed by Lukas von
Hildebrandt, but subsequently much
altered. In 1945 the Austrian resistance
movement began to operate secretly
against the Nazis here and subsequently
the building was used as a headquarters
by the military police of the allies under
the occupation.
*A short walk further north brings you to the
Josefstädter Strasse.*

4 THEATER IN DER JOSEFSTADT

Originally built in the 18th century,
the theatre at no 26 was remodelled
by Josef Kornhäusel. When it re–
opened in 1822 Beethoven conducted a
piece he had composed for the
inauguration.
*Turn right along Piaristengasse. On your
left you will shortly come to Jodok-Fink-
Platz.*

5 PIARISTENKIRCHE

The Piarist Church, which stands on the
south side of the square, is one of the
finest rococo churches in Vienna, built
principally to a design by Ignaz
Dientzenhofer in the mid-18th century
(see page 97). In 1861 the composer
Anton Bruckner underwent his
examination by professors of the Music
Academy here. After hearing him
demonstrate his prowess on the organ,
one of them remarked: 'He should be
examining us.'
*At the end of Piaristengasse turn right into
Florianigasse and almost immediately left
into Lange Gasse.*

6 PALAIS SCHÖNBORN

The original Schönborn Palace was
designed by Lukas von Hildebrandt,
who was employed by the powerful
Schönborn family as General Inspector
of their estates. When Lady Mary
Montagu wrote her impressions of
Vienna in 1716 she described this as one
of the most splendid palaces of the city.
Since 1920 the Museum für
Völkerkunde (Folklore Museum) has
been housed here.
*Return to Lange Gasse and cross Alser
Strasse into Spitalgasse.*

7 NARRENTURM

The huge complex of the Allgemeines
Krankenhaus (General Hospital)
contains a curiosity. The Narrenturm
(Idiots' Tower – access via Spitalgasse
23) is a cylindrical building originally
intended for the confinement of the
mentally ill. Unfortunately, some nobles
misused it for shutting up recalcitrant
sons who wouldn't marry the brides
selected for them. Housed within the
Narrenturm is the Museum of
Pathological Anatomy (see page 96).
*Walk back to Alser Strasse, and turn left for
Schottentor and trams.*

Theater in der Josefstadt

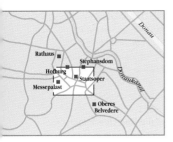

Cultural Metropolis

This walk encompasses some of the major shrines of art in Vienna. *Allow 1 hour (longer if touring the art collections)*

Start in the great square between the Naturhistorisches Museum and Kunsthistorisches Museum (Museums of Natural History and Art History) on the Burgring/Maria-Theresien-Platz.

Nearby

Messepalast

Hotel Imperial

1 KAISERIN-MARIA-THERESIA-DENKMAL

The huge monument to Maria Theresa stands in the middle of the square named after her. She sits on her throne holding the symbols of power and surrounded on the plinth below by her counsellors, administrators and generals.

2 NATURHISTORISCHES MUSEUM, KUNSTHISTORISCHES MUSEUM

These museums (see pages 76–7) contain collections founded by the Habsburg emperors. The original plan of architect Gottfried Semper was to unite the vast museum complex with

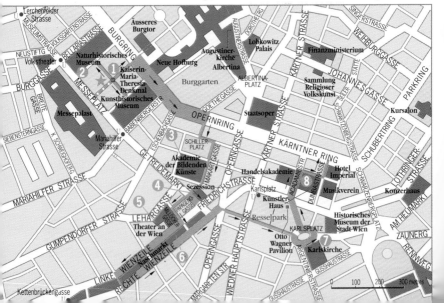

the Hofburg, in one great 'imperial forum'.

Walk east on the southern side of the Ring to Schillerplatz.

3 AKADEMIE DER BILDENDEN KÜNSTE

The Academy of Fine Arts along the south side of the square was built in 1877. Several famous artists fell out with the conservative professors and one aspirant was turned down – Adolf Hitler (see page 42).

Walk along Makartgasse beside the Academy and turn left.

4 SEZESSION

At Friedrichstrasse no 12 is the celebrated building of the Viennese Secession. In 1897 a group of artists broke away from the conservative Academy and commissioned Joseph Olbrich to build them their own exhibition hall. The irreverent Viennese refer to the gilded cupola of laurel leaves as the 'golden cabbage' (see pages 102–3).

Cross the Getreidemarkt at the junction and walk back up to Papagenogasse on your left which leads into Millöckergasse.

5 THEATER AN DER WIEN

Over the door of the entrance in Millöckergasse is a representation of Papageno (the bird-catcher in Mozart's opera *The Magic Flute*) playing his seductive tunes. This Papageno is actually Emanuel Schikaneder, the opera's librettist and owner-manager of the theatre. *The Magic Flute's* première took place in Schikaneder's previous establishment, but Beethoven's *Fidelio* was first performed here.

6 NASCHMARKT

Opposite the theatre, is the Naschmarkt (food market). This is always lively and has a flea market at one end on Saturdays.

Take the Rechte Wienzeile back to the junction with the Sezession; cross the Wiedner Hauptstrasse to the Resselpark.

7 KARLSKIRCHE

The east end of the Resselpark merges into Karlsplatz, on which stands the magnificent Karlskirche (Church of St Charles Borromeo), built by Fischer von Erlach, father and son. It is regarded as one of the finest baroque churches in Europe (see page 74).

Cross under the main artery to the north of Karlsplatz by Otto Wagner's elegant pavilion for the city railway.

8 KÜNSTLERHAUS, MUSIKVEREIN

The Künstlerhaus is used for exhibitions mostly staged by the Historisches Museum der Stadt Wien (Historical Museum of Vienna) diagonally opposite it on Karlsplatz (see page 64). The Musikverein, by Theophil Hansen, is the venue for the famous New Year's Day Concert of the Wiener Philharmonic.

Dumbastrasse leads back to the Ring past the Hotel Imperial, frequented by the famous and the infamous, including Richard Wagner and Adolf Hitler.

The baroque interior of the Karlskirche

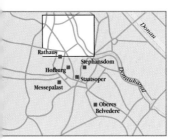

Architectural Kaleidoscope

This tour covers many different aspects and
periods of Vienna in one walk.
Allow 2 hours

*Begin at the major tram junction of Schottentor. Emerge from the
underpasses on to Rooseveltplatz.*

Nearby

Alservorstadt-

Pfarrkirche

Plaque

commemorating

Beethoven's death

1 VOTIVKIRCHE

In front of you is the impressive neo-gothic votive church
designed by Heinrich Ferstel and completed in 1879. It was
erected to commemorate Emperor Francis Joseph's lucky
escape from a knife attack by a Hungarian insurrectionist in
1853. Inside is the Renaissance tomb of Graf Salm, defender
of the city against the first Turkish attack in 1529 (see page
118).
Walk up Währinger Strasse to no 25 on the left.

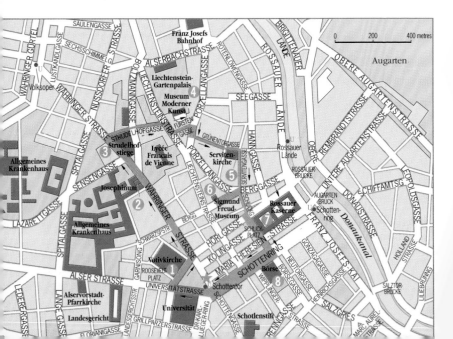

2 JOSEPHINUM

The building was erected under Joseph II. It contains not only a fine library with coffered ceiling and Corinthian columns, but also the famous wax models graphically illustrating all parts of the human body for instruction purposes. It is now partly a museum and partly annexed to the university (see page 74).
Turn right off Währinger Strasse further on at Strudelhofgasse.

3 STRUDELHOFSTIEGE

These magnificent art nouveau steps have been made famous by Heimito von Doderer's novel of the same name. They were built by Theodor Jäger in 1910 (see page 116).
The steps lead down to the Liechten-steinstrasse. Turn right along it and left into Fürstengasse for the palace entrance.

4 LIECHTENSTEIN-GARTENPALAIS

At Fürstengasse no 2 is the public access to the monumental palace built for the Liechtenstein family, and completed in 1704. The palace houses the Museum Moderner Kunst (Museum of Modern Art). The Liechtensteins' own art collection, said to have rivalled the emperor's, was moved to Vaduz during World War II and has since been much depleted by the sale of masterworks.
Leave the palace, turn right out of Fürstengasse into Porzellangasse, then left into Grünentorgasse. The second junction is Servitengasse.

5 SERVITENKIRCHE

The Servites were given permission by Ferdinand II to found a branch of the order in Vienna in 1636. Most of the elegant design is by Carlo Canevale, and is one of the few unified baroque

concepts to survive from before the Turkish siege of 1683. In the interior, under the towers, are two chapels with remarkable stucco work, especially that with scenes from the life of St John Nepomuk. The Peregrinus chapel, named after the Servite saint, was and is a pilgrimage shrine for those with foot ailments, among them Joseph Haydn.
Continue south along Servitengasse to the junction with Berggasse.

6 SIGMUND-FREUD-MUSEUM

At Berggasse no 19 is the apartment where Freud lived before being compelled to flee by the Nazis. He was obliged also to pay a surreal 'Tax on fleeing the German Reich' for the privilege of leaving. The apartment is now a museum (see page 103).
Retrace your steps to the junction of Berggasse, Porzellangasse, Servitengasse and Schlickgasse, and take the latter street.

7 ROSSAUER KASERNE

The huge Italianate barracks on Schlickplatz, known as the Rossauer Kaserne, are used by the police. Like the Arsenal, this building was the reaction to the events of the 1848 revolution which nearly toppled the Habsburgs. According to legend, the colonel and major who designed the building forgot to put any toilets in it, an indication perhaps of the general level of regard of the officer class for the troops.
Continue south as far as Schottenring and turn right.

8 BÖRSE

Theophil Hansen's Stock Exchange, on the far side of Schottenring at no 16, is now reviving after years of near inactivity (see page 52).
From here walk back to Schottentor.

Beethoven and Karl Marx

This walk traverses an elegant villa region, a park and a wine village associated with Beethoven.
Allow 1½ hours, plus ¼ hour if visiting the Beethoven memorial rooms

Nearby

Grinzing (Bus 38A from the junction between Armbrustergasse and Grinzinger Strasse)

Take Tram 37 from Schottentor and descend at Hohe Warte (last stop, actually on Wollergasse). The tram passes Schubert's birthplace on the right at Nussdorfer Strasse no 54.

1 VILLA COLONY

You alight just above the Zentralanstadt für Meteorologie und Geodynamik (Meteorological Office), with a fine view of the Leopoldsberg ahead in the distance. On the right, as you move round the corner from Wollergasse into Steinfeldgasse, is a villa colony. Note no 10 Wollergasse, which recalls the work of the Scottish architect Charles Rennie Mackintosh, who influenced the Viennese Secession. Most of these houses were built by Josef Hoffmann for the rich patrons of the Wiener Werkstätte and the Sezession. *Bear left off Steinfeldgasse into Heiligenstädter Park.*

2 HEILIGENSTÄDTER PARK

This picturesque park on a steeply sloping hillside is laid out in the English manner. A path winds down to the left passing a rather idealised statue of Beethoven by Robert Weigl (1910). Beethoven lived at two addresses near here, no 6 Probusgasse and no 2 Pfarrplatz. In front of you is the parish church of St Michael, the most notable feature of which is the deep blue of the modern stained glass windows. *Go up Armbrustergasse and turn right into Probusgasse.*

3 BEETHOVEN HAUS

Armbrustergasse contains some pleasant taverns selling wine from their own vineyards. Probusgasse is named after the Roman emperor, Marcus Aurelius Probus (3rd century AD), who is credited with reorganising and promoting viticulture in Austria. Beethoven lived at no 6 and wrote his famous *Heiligenstädter Testament* here in 1802, in which he movingly described the onset of his deafness. German speakers may read a copy of it displayed in the small museum in the house which also contains contemporary prints and other memorabilia. The house itself has a charming inner courtyard and incorporates elements of a much earlier medieval building (see page 84).

4 HEILIGENSTADT

The village takes its name of 'Saint's Town' from St Severin, who proclaimed the gospel along the Danube from Vienna to Passau in the 5th century. Like Grinzing, it was repeatedly destroyed by invaders and rebuilt. In 1781 a mineral spring was discovered and Beethoven in fact moved up here to enjoy its healing properties (see page 127).
Walk down Probusgasse to Pfarrplatz.

5 HEILIGENSTÄDTER KIRCHE/BEETHOVEN HAUS

The ancient Heiligenstädter (Church of St James) was originally Romanesque, and overbuilt subsequently in Gothic style. An empty grave inside is associated with St Severin, who is supposed to have had his hermitage in a nearby vineyard. Next to the church is another house associated with Beethoven (Pfarrplatz no 2), who lived here briefly in the summer of 1817. It is now an attractive wine tavern with a garden at the rear.
Either follow the chestnut-and-acacia-flanked Eroicagasse, crossing the former cogwheel railway, and turn right down Beethovengang, at the bottom of which is the end-stop for Tram D; or leave Pfarrplatz by Nestelbachgasse, turn left into Grinzinger Strasse and walk down to the junction with Heiligenstädter Strasse.

Impressive Karl-Marx-Hof

6 KARL-MARX-HOF

Stretching for 1km from nos 82–92 of Heiligenstädter Strasse is the most remarkable building erected during the interwar period of 'Red Vienna', when the Social Democrats controlled City Hall. Designed by Karl Ehn, the Karl-Marx-Hof was an ambitious social housing project originally containing 1,325 apartments, together with almost all necessary ancillary services from laundry to surgeries and a post-office. Recently the whole complex has been listed for protection and upgraded.
Tram D takes you back to Schottentor.

A Villa, a Village and a View...

This rural route includes a walk round a park and through several attractive wine villages. *Allow 1¹/₂ hours, excluding a tour of the Geymüller-schlössel. If the extension to Bellevuehöhe is taken, allot a whole morning or afternoon*

Nearby

Römischer Kaiser,

Neustift am Walde

(restaurant – open:

Thursday to Monday

9am–11pm).

Take Tram 41 from Schottentor to the end stop at Pötzleinsdorf. On your left is the entrance to the park.

1 PÖTZLEINSDORFER SCHLOSSPARK

This sumptuous park was originally laid out for the Pötzleinsdorfer Schloss, which is now a Rudolf Steiner school. It was planned after the English manner by Konrad Rosenthal, a justly famous gardener in the employ of Prince Rasumofsky (who in turn is celebrated for commissioning Beethoven to

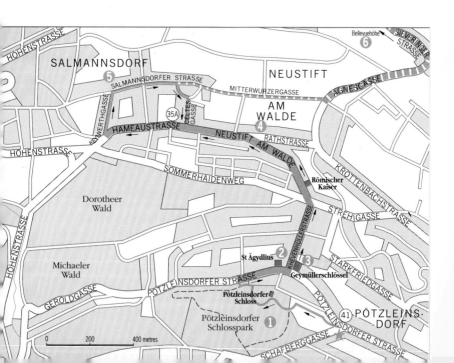

write some of his loveliest music for strings). A sort of summer house in the park is known as the 'Preindl Salettl' after Maria Preindl, one of the most famous courtesans of the Congress of Vienna, and lover of the Schloss's owner. *Leave the Schlosspark after walking some way past the duck pond (always keeping the high ground to your left), exiting by a gate into Pötzleinsdorfer Strasse and turning right.*

2 ST ÄGYDIUS

Walking down the street you come to the little baroque parish church with rich interior statuary and stucco-lustro decoration.

3 GEYMÜLLERSCHLÖSSEL

Opposite St Ägydius is the charming late-empire country house built for Baron Johann Heinrich Geymüller around 1808 (entrance at Khevenhüller-strasse no 2). Geymüller was banker to Emperor Francis I and helped him out with vast loans and donations during the war against Napoleon. The family were also industrialists and patrons of culture – in their city palace the cream of society and the arts used to meet in the years following the Congress of Vienna. The Schlössel is now run by the Österreich-isches Museum für Angewandte Kunst (Austrian Museum of Applied Arts) and contains a fine collection of Biedermeier furniture and 200 clocks mostly dating from 1780 to 1850. *After leaving the Schlössel, turn right out of the gate and walk up Khevenhüllerstrasse.*

4 NEUSTIFT AM WALDE

Continuing over the hill you descend into the enchanting wine village of Neustift am Walde. The picturesque name comes from the fact that the village was once in the possession of the 'new convent' of the Dorothean order located 'by the woods'. Later, like other villages and properties in the area, it came into the possession of the powerful monastery of Klosterneuburg on the Danube. The streets of Neustift am Walde, and Rathstrasse, which it joins, are lined with congenial wine taverns, most with terraced gardens at the back (see page 127). *Continue up Neustift am Walde and Hameaustrasse, then turn right up Keylwerthgasse, which leads into the adjoining village of Salmannsdorf.*

5 SALMANNSDORF

This is one of the most favoured *Heurigenorte* or wine-tavern villages. Around the western edge of Salmanns-dorf runs the famous Höhenstrasse that leads up to the viewpoints of the Kahlenberg and Leopoldsberg. This was built primarily as a measure to combat unemployment in the 1930s, but also had the useful function of linking the excursion areas of the western Vienna Woods (see page 127). *You can now either descend to Neustift am Walde via Celtesgasse and take Bus 35A to Nussdorfer Strasse, changing there for Tram 38 to Schottentor; or proceed along Salmannsdorfer Strasse, and Mitterwurzergasse, turn left up Agnesgasse, left again up Sieveringer Strasse, right up Gspöttgraben, and right into Himmelstrasse.*

6 BELLEVUEHÖHE

A memorial slab on this hilltop with a fine view of the city recalls that Sigmund Freud first formulated his ideas for *The Interpretation of Dreams* in a hotel that used to stand here (see page 129). *Himmelstrasse leads to Grinzing and the tram back to the city.*

What to See

AKADEMIE DER BILDENDEN KÜNSTE (Academy of Fine Arts)
This fine neo-Renaissance building was designed by Theophil Hansen in 1876. It has many attractive features, in particular the frescos of mythological scenes on the ceiling of the lobby by Anselm Feuerbach. The small, but exceptionally high quality gallery contains 17th-century works by Dutch and Flemish masters and a celebrated *Last Judgement* by Hieronymus Bosch. As a penniless young man, Adolf Hitler spent a miserable nine years in Vienna, struggling to become an artist. In 1907, at the age of 18, he failed the entry exam for the Academy. The examiners thought his architectural drawings were acceptable, but that he had submitted 'too few heads' (see page 35).
Schillerplatz 3. Tel: 588 16–0. Open: Tuesday, Thursday and Friday 10am–2pm; Wednesday 10am–1pm and 3pm–6pm; weekend 9am–1pm. Admission charge. Trams 1 and 2; U1, U2, U4 to Karlsplatz/Oper.

AKADEMIE DER WISSENSCHAFTEN (Academy of Sciences)
Franz Stephan, Holy Roman Emperor and husband of Maria Theresa, brought the architect Jean Nicolas Jadot de Ville-Issey from his homeland of Lorraine to Vienna. The former assembly hall of the Old University (now the Academy of Sciences) was built to his design between 1753 and 1755. A serious fire in 1961 destroyed the original ceiling frescos by Gregorio Guglielmi, since replaced by a copy. The interior is not normally accessible to the public (see page 29).
Dr-Ignaz-Seipel-Platz 2. Trams 1 and 2; U3 to Dr-Karl-Lueger-Platz/Stubentor.

ALBERTINA
The original building dates to 1781, with extensions built by Louis de Montoyer between 1801 and 1804, to incorporate parts of the old monastery of the Augustinians. The Albertina houses the greatest collection of drawings and graphics in the world, in total more than 220,000 items. There is a permanent rolling exhibition of drawings from the collection (see page 26).
Augustinerstrasse. Tel: 534 83. Open: Monday, Tuesday and Thursday 10am–4pm; Wednesday 10am–6pm; Friday 10am–2pm; weekend 10am–1pm. Closed Sunday in July and August. Admission charge. Trams 1 or 2; U1, U2, U4 to Karlsplatz/Oper.

ALPENGARTEN (Alpine Garden)
The oldest Alpine Garden in Europe has been laid out here in a part of the Botanical Garden, with artificially created alpine conditions. There are many hundreds of plants and a herb collection (see page 52).
Entrance from Landstrasser Gürtel or through the Botanical Garden, Mechelgasse 2. Tel: 78 31 49. Open: April to June, Monday to Friday 10am–6pm; weekends and holidays 9am–6pm. July to August, Monday to Friday 10am–4pm; weekends and holidays 9am–4pm. Admission charge. Tram 71 to Ungargasse.

ALTE UNIVERSITÄT (Old University)

Emperor Ferdinand II handed over control of the Vienna University to the Jesuits as part of the campaign to anchor the Counter-Reformation in the Habsburg domains. Between 1623 and 1627, and again in the 18th century, the existing building was altered and expanded. It now houses the Academy of Sciences (see page 29).

Dr-Ignaz-Seipel-Platz 1. Trams 1 and 2, U3 to Dr.-Karl-Lueger-Platz/ Stubenring.

ALTES RATHAUS (Former City Hall)

When a conspiracy of patrician Viennese families against the Habsburgs miscarried in 1309, one of the conspirators' houses was confiscated and the first council proceedings were held here in 1316. The building was altered and extended several times, and the baroque façade in the style of J B Fischer von Erlach was added in 1699. In the courtyard is one of Georg Raphael Donner's last works, the Andromeda Fountain dating from 1741.

The last council meeting was held here in 1885. The building now houses offices of the district administration, the District Museum and Museum of the Austrian Resistance Movement (see page 25).

Wipplingerstrasse 8. Tel 534 36/739. Open: Monday, Wednesday and Thursday 9am–5pm. Admission charge. Trams 1 and 2 to Börse.

AMALIENBAD

Otto Nadel and Karl Schmallhofer designed this fabulous glass-roofed swimming pool, with ancillary medicinal and steam baths, in 1926. The exterior is

The well at the Altes Rathaus

severely functional, in keeping with the modernist principles adhered to by the city planners of 'Red Vienna' in the 1920s and early 30s.

Reumannplatz 23. Tel: 601 12–0. Open: Tuesday 9am–5pm; Wednesday and Friday 9am–8.30pm; Thursday 7am–8.30pm; Saturday 7am–7pm; Sunday 7am–5pm. Admission charge. U1 to Reumannplatz.

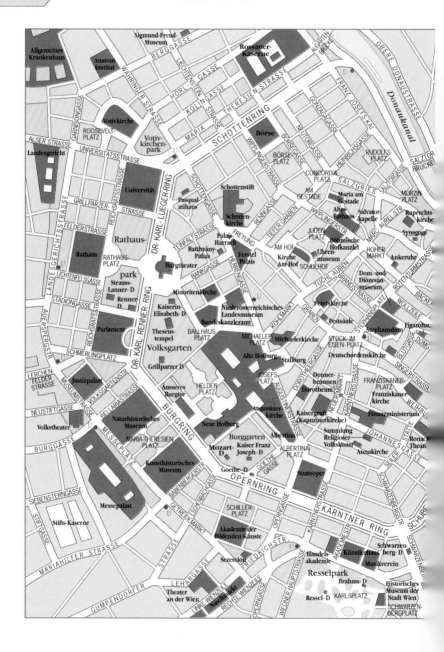

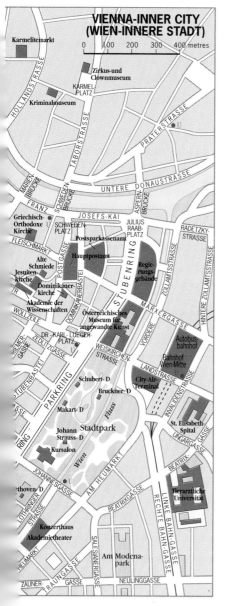

VIENNA-INNER CITY (WIEN-INNERE STADT)

0   100   200   300   400 metres

Karmelitemarkt

Zirkus-und Clownmuseum

KARMEL-PLATZ

Kriminalmuseum

HOLLANDSTRASSE

TABORSTRASSE

PRATERSTRASSE

UNTERE DONAUSTRASSE

ASPERN-BRÜCKE

SCHWEDEN-BRÜCKE

MARIEN-BRÜCKE

FRANZ

Griechisch-Orthodoxe Kirche

JOSEFS-KAI

SCHWEDEN-PLATZ

JULIUS RAAB-PLATZ

RADETZKY-STRASSE

FLEISCHMARKT

Postsparkassenamt

Alte Schmiede

Hauptpostamt

Jesuiten-kirche

Dominikaner-kirche

Akademie der Wissenschaften

Österreichisches Museum für angewandte Kunst

DOMINIKANERBASTEI

POSTGASSE

STUBENRING

Regierungs-gebäude

ZOLLAMTSSTRASSE

HINTERE ZOLLAMTSSTRASSE

WOLLZEILE

MARXERGASSE

DR. KARL-LUEGER-PLATZ

RIEMER-GASSE

ZEDLITZGASSE

WEISKIRCHEN-STRASSE

VORDERE

Autobus bahnhof

Bahnhof Wien-Mitte

LANDSTRASSE

STUBENBASTEI

PARKRING

Schubert- D

City-Air Terminal

Bruckner- D

Makart- D

Wien

INVALIDENSTRASSE

St. Elisabeth Spital

UNGARGASSE

RING

Johann Stadtpark Strauss- D

Kursalon

AM HEUMARKT

BEATRIX-

BEATRIXGASSE

Tierärztliche Universität

JOHANNESGASSE

-thoven- D

LOTHRINGER-STRASSE

Konzerthaus

Akademietheater

SALESIANERGASSE

RECHTE BAHNGASSE

LINKE BAHNGASSE

Am Modena-park

HEUMARKT

ZAUNER-GASSE

TRAUNGASSE

NEULINGGASSE

ANKER CLOCK

The clock brightens up the bridge between the two buildings belonging to the Anker Insurance Company. Franz Matsch created it to an art nouveau design between 1911 and 1917. The idea was to unveil it at the appropriate moment as a monument to the victory of the Austro-Hungarian Empire in World War I. This victory not forthcoming, it was some time before the authorities decided they might as well unveil it anyway. Through the hours 12 figures, or pairs of figures, move across the clock-face, which shows the ancient coat of arms of Vienna. The historical characters begin with Marcus Aurelius and end with Joseph Haydn. At midday all the figures parade round in sequence (see page 25).

Hoher Markt 10-11. Trams 1 and 2; U1 and U4 to Schwedenplatz.

ARSENAL

After the citizens plundered the Civil Armoury 'Am Hof' in the revolution of 1848, the Arsenal was built, partly as a depository for weapons, partly as a production centre for war materials. The striking Italianate romantic aspect of the buildings is shared by one or two other military establishments of the same period. Inside the complex is the Heeresgeschichtliches Museum (Museum of Military History). A colossal allegory of Austria in marble by J Benk crowns the stairs. One room is devoted to Archduke Franz Ferdinand and his assassination in Sarajevo (see page 31).

Arsenalstrasse. Tel: 78 23 03. Open: daily 10am–4pm. Closed: Friday. Admission charge. Trams D or 18 to Schweizergarten.

Vienna

A meeting point between East and West

Vienna has always been cosmopolitan and multicultural, yet at the same time unmistakably and homogeneously 'Viennese'. Traditionally, immigration came from the East, from the far-flung lands of the Habsburg Empire. Long-established ethnic restaurants are reminders of this – the Ilona-Stüberl in the Bräunerstrasse, for example, where not only typical Hungarian cuisine is on offer, but also typical Hungarian helpings. In the same street is the Bukarest (Romanian, as the name implies) and in the Naglergasse is the Serbian Budva. The post-war population of *Gastarbeiter* have added to the scene, with their grocery shops and kebab houses.

Politically and diplomatically Vienna has straddled East and West since the war, exploiting Austria's neutral status. Beneath the surface, spying and smuggling thrived when the Iron Curtain divided Europe; at the same time, the city was the venue for summit meetings, like that between Kennedy and Kruschev in 1961, and Carter and Brezhnev in 1979.

Not only spies and diplomats found and find fertile ground here for their manoeuvring: since 1979, when 'UNO-City' was opened on the Danube, international civil servants have poured in to staff the United Nations Development Agency, the UNRWA, the UNFOAC, and other agencies such as OPEC. East and West and the Third World rub shoulders in a city that manages to be provincial and international at the same time.

Taking it easy: don't rush the sights

A fiaker is the only way to see this historic city

Kaffeehaus in the Graben

Belvedere

*A*lthough Prince Eugene of Savoy, the most celebrated of the Habsburg generals, had planned a 'Garden Palace' as early as 1697, the money for it was not available until Emperor Charles VI paid him the promised honorarium for his victories in the War of the Spanish Succession (1701–14). On receipt of this, together with his salary as Regent of the Spanish Netherlands and further imperial rewards, the Prince was in a position to put in hand one of the most ambitious building projects ever undertaken by a private individual before the age of millionaire businessmen.

When the whole complex of Lower and Upper Belvedere with the luxurious baroque garden was complete, a visiting French nobleman observed dryly that it was delightful to see how 'in Austria the subjects of the emperor lived more splendidly than the emperor himself'.

Home to Austria's modern art, the Upper Belvedere is an imposing baroque palace

UNTERES BELVEDERE (Lower Belvedere)

The building of the Lower Palace to plans by Lukas von Hildebrandt was begun in 1714 and completed in 1716 –

a remarkably rapid rate of progress by the standards of the day. This part of the palace was destined for living quarters and administrative offices for the Prince's estates, to which was attached an Orangery (since all self-respecting French palaces had one).

The interior of the Lower Belvedere

is worth visiting for itself, although it also contains the Österreichisches Barockmuseum (Austrian Baroque Museum), part of the Austrian Gallery. It is an elegant long and low baroque palace, with huge windows reaching almost the ground. The two-storeyed middle part contains the 'marble hall', with a spectacular ceiling fresco by Martin Altomonte showing the 'Apotheosis' of Prince Eugene after the victory over the Turks at Peterwardein (Serbia).

Österreichisches Barockmuseum (Austrian Baroque Museum)

The star items in the collection are the original of Georg Raphael Donner's Providentia (Providence) Fountain on the Neuer Markt, and the extraordinary busts by Franz Xaver Messerschmidt, the features of which are stamped with grotesque grimaces. Besides high quality portraits of the baroque nobility, there are also busts of Emperor Franz I and of Maria Theresa; also a marble sculpture, again showing the 'Apotheosis' of Prince Eugene, by Balthasar Permoser. Many of the artists represented here gained the major commissions for decorating contemporary churches in Vienna, so that the works of, for example, Johann Michael Rottmayr, Daniel Gran, Paul Troger, Martino Altomonte and Franz Anton Maulbertsch will seem to be all around you as you tour the city.

Medieval Art in the Orangery

The gallery contains medieval religious paintings from all over Austria, with the west and Tyrol being particularly generously represented. There are a number of wood sculptures, some polychromed.

The Gardens

Between 1721 and 1723 the Bavarian Dominique Girard worked for Prince Eugene on the gardens, having been loaned by his employer, Max Emanuel of Bavaria. They were laid out in classical French manner, geometrically divided with paths, and incorporating waterworks and a labyrinth.

Tel: 78 41 58–0. Opening times for the Upper Belvedere and Lower Belvedere are the same: Tuesday to Sunday 10am–5pm. Admission charge. The Lower Belvedere houses the Austrian Baroque Museum and the Museum of Medieval Austrian Art (in the Orangery). The Upper Belvedere contains the Austrian Gallery of 19th- and 20th-Century Art, together with a temporary display of 19th- and 20th-century European painting (see page 31).

Entrances at Rennweg 6, Landstrasser Gürtel and Prinz-Eugen-Strasse 27. Tram D to Prinz-Eugen-Strasse, Tram 71 to Salesianergasse, both from Schwarzenbergplatz.

Impressive stairway in the Belvedere

The impressive baroque façade of Prince Eugene's ceremonial palace

OBERES BELVEDERE (Upper Belvedere)

In order to ensure a sufficiently noble view, Prince Eugene persuaded his neighbour, Prince Schwarzenberg, to cede part of his garden next door, and only when these delicate negotiations had been concluded could he give the order to begin building. Originally, a comparatively modest palace had been planned, but at an early stage the Prince seems to have changed his mind, perhaps persuaded by his architect Hildebrandt, perhaps finding the generosity of his imperial benefactor greater than expected. The result is one of the grandest and most lovely represen-tational baroque palaces ever built.

The layout

Hildebrandt made adept use of the height differences of the site, so that the southern side of the palace is half a storey lower, and the ground-floor windows on the garden side are thus effectively half subterranean. In the middle, where the entrance has now been built in, there was originally an arcade right through the building for carriages. This alteration was made when Emperor Joseph II moved the Imperial Picture Collection from the Stallburg to the Belvedere in 1775. In 1783 it was the first collection in the world to boast a scientific catalogue and the first also to offer free access to the public. In 1892 the pictures were transferred to the newly built Kunsthistorisches Museum (Museum of Fine Arts) on the Ringstrasse.

Rival court

The last time the palace was used as a residency was in the early years of this century. Archduke Franz Ferdinand, nephew of Emperor Francis Joseph and heir to the throne, set up a rival court here to his ageing uncle in the Hofburg, and tried to pursue his own political and diplomatic aims. His assassination at Sarajevo in 1914 put an abrupt end to these machinations.

Signing of the State Treaty

In 1955 the Upper Belvedere was the scene of rejoicing when the State Treaty was signed with the four powers who had occupied Austria since the end of World War II. In the marble hall, Dulles (US), Macmillan (UK), Molotov (USSR) and Pinay (France) put their signatures to the document, which was then displayed from the balcony to the cheering crowds.

Entry is via the impressive Sala Terrena, the vaulted roof of which is supported by pillars in the form of Atlas figures. The noble stairway leads to the magnificent Ceremonial Room, where there is also a painting of the 1955 signing ceremony. On the various floors of the Belvedere are located different sections of the Austrian Gallery.

Österreichische Galerie (Austrian Art Gallery)

This was intended to show only Austrian works, but at present it also temporarily accommodates (on the ground floor) European works from the 19th and early 20th century, that formerly constituted the Neue Galerie in the Stallburg.

On the first floor are works by artists of the Biedermeier period (1814–48) including Ferdinand Georg Waldmüller, Friedrich von Amerling and Peter Fendi. These are mostly somewhat idealised

Example of the Belvedere's garden statuary

depictions of bourgeois family life, though social realism is also evident, particularly in Fendi's work. There are also marvellous views of Vienna by the Alt painter dynasty, and historicist works by the most fashionable painter of the late 19th century, Hans Makart.

On the second floor are the works of the Secessionist painters, in particular Gustav Klimt, and the Austrian Expressionists, such as Egon Schiele and Oskar Kokoschka. In recent years these artists have become extremely well-known outside Austria as a result of the large-scale exhibitions of turn-of-the-century culture and politics. Works like Klimt's *The Kiss* or Egon Schiele's *Death and the Maiden* have come to seem emblematic of reactions to the ages prevailing ethos.

BÖHMISCHE HOFKANZLEI
(Former Bohemian Chancellery)

Fischer von Erlach the Elder designed the building, which was completed in 1714, and Matthias Gerl subsequently extended it. The coats of arms of Bohemia, Moravia and Silesia may be seen on the façade. As a result of Maria Theresa's administrative reforms the Bohemian Chancellery was merged with other organs of government in 1749. It was badly damaged in the war and extensive reconstruction was needed. It is now the seat of the Administrative and Constitutional Courts and is not therefore accessible to sightseers (see page 25).
Wipplingerstrasse 7, Judenplatz 11. Trams 1 and 2 to Börse.

The baroque Böhmische Hofkanzlei

BÖRSE (Stock Exchange)

This is one of the more elegant buildings of the so-called *Gründerzeit* (literally 'foundation period' of the mid- to late 19th century, when finance and industry were being transformed in the Austrian lands). Theophil Hansen designed it in neo-Renaissance style, using marble, cool grey stone and red brick from the Wienerberg. It was completed in 1877, and severely damaged by fire in 1956, but has since been restored. It still houses the Austrian stock exchange (see page 37).
Schottenring 16. Trams 1 and 2.

Sculptures atop the Böhmische Hofkanzlei

BOTANISCHER GARTEN DER UNIVERSITÄT (Botanical Gardens)

Maria Theresa's physician, Van Swieten, advised the systematic planting of medicinal herbs, and the Empress donated the resulting garden to the University in 1757 (see Alpengarten page 42).
Mechelgasse 2, near Rennweg. Tel: 78 71 01. Open: mid-April to mid-October, daily 10am to dusk. Tram 71 to Ungargasse.

_If you speak German you must not miss
the Burgtheater experience_

BÜRGERLICHES ZEUGHAUS (Former Citizens' Armoury)

The long, narrow building of the Citizens' Armoury was provided with a somewhat grandiose baroque façade by the architect Anton Ospel when he rebuilt it in 1732 after the Turkish siege of 1683.

In the revolution of 1848 the students were supplied with weapons from here and for a while it served as headquarters for the revolutionary National Guard. It is now the headquarters of the fire brigade, the entrance to whose museum is at Am Hof 7(see page 25).
Am Hof 10 (to visit tel: 531 99). Trams 1 and 2 to Schottentor .

BURGTHEATER (National Theatre)

Gottfried Semper and Karl von Hasenauer collaborated on the design of this neo-baroque theatre to replace the old Burgtheater, which stood on the Michaelerplatz. Gustav Klimt, his brother Ernst and Franz Matsch painted the frescos on the stairways; they represent theatre history from earliest times.

Like the Opera House, the building was seriously damaged during World War II. It has a long and famous tradition and is still considered to be among the best in the German-speaking world (see page 22).
Dr-Karl-Lueger-Ring 2 (for times of guided tours of the interior tel: 514 44–2182). Trams 1 and 2.

Cafés

A Viennese newspaper article in 1972 attributed the tripling of the use of tranquillisers in the previous six years largely to the decline of the coffee-house, the place where traditionally one could do one's grumbling to a sympathetic audience. Some people attribute the rise of the coffee-house culture to the formerly unappealing nature of so many Viennese homes – dark, dank and impregnated with other people's cooking smells. The writer Peter Altenberg actually gave his preferred coffee-house as his address, often deserting it only to sleep at the nearby Graben Hotel.

In those days, the coffee-houses were male chauvinist sanctuaries, but after World War I women – and even married couples – put an end to that. 'For ten years' wrote Alfred Polgar, 'the two of them sat for hours every day quite alone in a coffee house. That is a good marriage, you will say! No. That is a good coffee-house!'

Although Hawelka maintains the Bohemian tradition, it has to be admitted that the literary café is largely a thing of the past. What remains is the tendency of individual cafés to attract a particular clientele – politicians and officials from the nearby ministries favour Landtmann, while Tirolerhof is still something of a women's locale.

Thankfully, the decline of the café has been halted, and they again fulfil their essential role: a place to meet one's friends, eat cheaply, idle the time away, and read the newspapers. As Peter Altenberg put it: 'a place for people who want to be alone, but who need society to achieve this'.

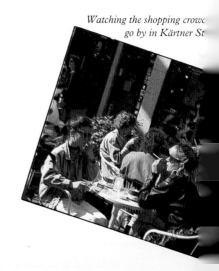

Watching the shopping crowds go by in Kärtner St

Indulge yourself with
Sachertorte and coffee

Admire the wonderful
view of Stephansdom over
your coffee at the Hass haus

Observe the Bohemian
life-style from the Café Hawelka

Inner City Churches

Early baroque Dominikanerkirche

ANNAKIRCHE (St Anne's Church)
This baroque jewel in the heart of the
city is built on the site of the 16th-
century chapel which served the
Clarissan convent adjoining it. Rudolf II
bestowed both the church and cloister
on the Jesuits, who later erected a
novitiate's house here. In the mid-18th
century the church was substantially
rebuilt after a fire and the present lavish
baroque decoration installed. The ceiling
fresco and the altar picture of the Holy

Trinity are by Daniel Gran. In a side-
chapel is an important work attributed to
Veit Stoß of Nürnberg, a wooden
sculpture of Mary and Jesus with Anne,
mother of Mary.
*Annagasse 3b. Trams 1 and 2 and U1, U2,
U4 to Karlsplatz/Oper.*

**AUGUSTINERKIRCHE
(Church of the Augustinian Friary)**
This Gothic church dates to 1338, when
it was erected for the monastery of the
Augustinian friars. It has seen many
spectacular Habsburg marriages, in
particular that of Maria Theresa to
Franz Stephan of Lorraine, and of her
daughter Marie Antoinette to the future
Louis XVI (by proxy). Another
politically inspired marriage was that of
the daughter of Franz I to Napoleon.
The most famous monument inside is
the cenotaph of Maria Theresa's
daughter Marie Christine by Antonio
Canova (1805). The hearts of the
Habsburgs are preserved in silver urns in
the Heart Vault (see page 26).
*Augustinerstrasse 3. Entrance from
Josefsplatz. Trams 1 and 2, U1, U2, U4 to
Karlsplatz/Oper.*

**DEUTSCHORDENSHAUS UND
KIRCHE (The House and Church of
the Teutonic Order)**
The Teutonic Knights were founded
during the Third Crusade and provided
a hospital service during the Siege of
Acre (1190). Their Viennese church
goes back to 1326, although they were
settled here as early as 1120. There are
some fine monuments to members of the
order inside the little Gothic church.

A lift on the edge of the attractive inner courtyard beyond the church gives access to the Schatzkammer des Deutschen Ordens (Treasury of the Order of Teutonic Knights). The collection contains artefacts, insignia and memorial portraits relating to the order.
Singerstrasse 7. Tel: 512 10 65/6. Open: varies, check before visiting. Admission charge. U1 and U3 to Stephansplatz.

DOMINIKANERKIRCHE (Dominican Church)

The Dominicans were called to Vienna as early as 1226 by the Babenberg Duke Leopold VI. There had been two churches on this site (one Romanesque, one Gothic) before the present baroque church was built in 1634 by Jakob Spatz, Cipriano Biasino and Antonio Canevale. The ivy-covered monastery adjoining it was built at the same time. The interior presents a unified baroque concept, realised through stucco, frescos and paintings. Notable is Tobias Pock's depiction in the right-hand aisle's altar of St Dominic himself and the Trinity. The Dominicans, 'Hounds of the Lord', were noted for their intellectual distinction (see page 29).
Postgasse 4. Trams 1 and 2 and U3 to Stubentor.

FRANZISKANERKIRCHE (Franciscan church)

In 1589 the Franciscans took over the former 'penitents' house' for reformed prostitutes, which had a small chapel attached. The façade of the early 17th-century church combines south German Renaissance features with Gothic. Over the altar is a striking illusionist painting by Andrea Pozzo (1707).
Franziskanerplatz. U1 and U3 to Stephansplatz.

GRIECHISCH-ORTHODOXE KIRCHE (Greek Orthodox Church)

A Greek Orthodox community was founded in Vienna in the late 18th century, taking advantage of Emperor Joseph II's Edict of Tolerance (1781) which allowed non-Catholics to build churches and practise their faiths freely without fear.

In the 19th century the wealthy Greek financier, Baron Sina, commissioned Theophil Hansen to redesign the modest building they had on the Fleischmarkt. He produced this wonderful Byzantine imitation, whose interior is pleasingly lavish, with gilded marble columns, vaulted ceilings with frescos, and a fine iconostasis (see page 29).
Fleischmarkt 15. Trams 1 and 2, U1 and U4 to Schwedenplatz.

Mollner's original Griechisch-Orthodoxe Kirche was improved when Hansen imposed Byzantine–style renovations

The sober façade of Jesuitenkirche

JESUITENKIRCHE (Jesuit Church or University Church)

When the Jesuits took over responsibility for the University in 1623, Ferdinand II also required that they build a church for it. This later church was built in 1705. The relatively restrained façade hardly prepares one for the showy Jesuitical pomp of the interior, for the spectacular theatrical effects of which Andrea Pozzo and his workshop were responsible. A further touch of grandeur is given by the lustrous curlicue columns, a direct allusion to those of St Peter's in Rome (see page 29).

Dr-Ignaz-Seipel-Platz. Trams 1 and 2, U3 to Dr-Karl-Lueger-Platz/Stubentor.

KAPUZINERKIRCHE UND KAPUZINERGRUFT (Capuchin Church and Crypt)

The crypt of the modest Capuchin Church was the Imperial burial vault for the Habsburgs from 1633 to the end of their dynasty's rule. The most impressive tomb is Balthasar Moll's double sarcophagus for Maria Theresa and her husband Franz Stephan. The crypt exudes a powerful atmosphere of *memento mori*, entirely appropriate to the somewhat macabre religiosity of the Habsburgs. The custom was for their hearts to be preserved in the Augustinerkirche, their entrails in the catacombs of St Stephen's and the rest of them here (see page 114).

Neuer Markt. Crypt open daily 9.30am–4pm. Admission charge. Trams 1 and 2; U1, U2 and U4 to Karlsplatz/Oper.

KIRCHE AM HOF (Am Hof Church)

The baroque former Jesuit Church of the Nine Choirs of Angels is built on an ancient site and incorporates elements of an earlier Gothic church belonging to the Carmelites. Before that the Ducal Mint was here, itself occupying the premises formerly constituting the court of the Babenbergs. From the balcony the end of the Holy Roman Empire was announced in 1806 – a move forced on Francis I by Napoleon. Thereafter the Habsburgs remained simply Emperors of Austria. The façade is by Carlo Carlone (1662); the coffered ceiling inside and classical choir were features added in the late 18th century. Frescos in the side chapels are by Franz Anton Maulbertsch and others, but in poor condition (see page 25)

Am Hof. Trams 1 and 2, U2 to Schottentor, U3 to Herrengasse.

The Michaelerkirche from the Platz

MARIA AM GESTADE (Church of 'Mary on the River Bank')

This remarkable Gothic church with its narrow, soaring façade and unmistakable filigree steeple is one of the finest surviving pieces of 14th-century architecture in the city. The architect was Michael Knab, who had to wrestle with the problem of the precarious site, which fell away sharply to the Danube on one side. The highly noticeable result is that the nave is smaller than the choir, and the two are not aligned. The church has survived much: it was damaged during the Turkish siege, and Joseph II considered turning it into a pawn shop; in the Napoleonic Wars it was used as a store, and even as a stable for cavalry horses. Subsequently it became associated with Clemens Maria Hofbauer, leader of the proselytising Redemptorist Order in 19th-century Austria. His tomb can be seen in the church (see page 25).

Am Gestade. Trams 1 and 2 to Börse.

MICHAELERKIRCHE (St Michael's Church)

This ancient Gothic church was built in the late 14th century, incorporating elements of an even earlier Romanesque building. The oldest parts are the choir, the side-aisle (St Nicholas Chapel) with stone figures dating back to 1350 and the lower half of the octagonal tower. The tower chapel contains the remnants of late Romanesque frescos. In the 17th and 18th century it acquired its baroque features. Particularly striking is the stucco relief of the fall of the angels behind the high altar. In 1724 the portal was added to the main entrance and Lorenzo Mattielli's dramatic statuary of St Michael casting out a rebellious angel was subsequently placed above it. The neoclassical façade was made in 1792. St Michael's was a burial church, and there are tombs and memorials to prominent Habsburg loyalists in the interior. Pietro Metastasio, court poet to Charles VI and Maria Theresa is buried in the crypt (see page 23).

Michaelerplatz. U3 to Herrengasse.

MINORITENKIRCHE (Church of the Minorites)

The minor order of the Franciscans came to Vienna in 1230 and built themselves a monastery and church. In the chapter-house of the latter the defeated king of Bohemia was laid out in 1278 and the victor, Rudolf of Habsburg, inducted into the order. The Gothic core of the present church dates to 1380, and is attributed to a monkish master-builder, 'Father James of Paris'. The fine sculptural reliefs on the west portals, (*The Crucifixion, A Madonna with Child, St Francis receiving the*

Stigmata), are attributed to him. Between 1784 and 1789 Ferdinand von Hohenberg 're-gothicised' the church, stripping out the baroque fittings of the Counter-Reformation, and adding a neo-gothic pulpit, organ loft, and high altar. On the north wall is a huge tasteless mosaic, Giacomo Raffaelli's copy of Leonardo da Vinci's *The Last Supper*, originally commissioned by Napoleon and briefly misplaced and rediscovered having been stored at the Belvedere (see page 23).
Minoritenplatz. U3 to Herrengasse.

PETERSKIRCHE (St Peter's Church)

By tradition the first church of Vienna, built in Roman times, stood on the site of Lukas von Hildebrandt's superb baroque church, constructed mostly between 1703 and 1708. It displays to good advantage the architect's skill at fitting a massive and monumental building into a comparatively narrow space. The highlights of the elongated oval of the interior, with its majestic cupola above, are the frescos and the gilded stucco. *The Assumption of Mary* in the cupola was painted by Johann Michael Rottmayr (1714); the marvellous baroque carving of the pulpit is by Matthias Steindl, and that of the drowning of St John Nepomuk in the Moldau (on the right of the nave) probably by Lorenzo Mattielli. The high altar was designed by the Italian master of theatre architecture, Antonio Galli-Bibiena (see page 27).
Petersplatz. U 1 and U2 to Stephans-platz.

Modelled on St Peter's in Rome, Peterskirche was cleverly squeezed on to the historic site by Hildebrandt

RUPRECHTSKIRCHE (St Rupert's Church)

While the first church on the site of St Peter's was the earliest in Vienna, St Rupert's Church is the oldest still standing. It is a modest, architecturally undistinguished building which originally stood against the city wall, with a steep drop to the Danube below it. At this point of the river there were wharves for the ships that brought salt from the *Salzkammergut*, the salt mines of western Austria. St Rupert is the patron saint of the miners and many small alpine churches of similar character are also dedicated to him. In the early Christian period the churches of Vienna were mostly within the bounds of the Salzburg diocese. The evocative interior of the ivy-covered church retains some traces of Romanesque; the aisle and lower part of the tower date to the 11th century (see page 25).

Ruprechtsplatz. Trams 1 and 2, U 1 and U4 to Schwedenplatz.

The Kaiser Monument stands before the misnamed Schottenkirche

SALVATORKAPELLE (Chapel of the Saviour)

The Salvatorkapelle is the focus of the Viennese 'Old Catholics' community, founded through rejection of the infallibility doctrine promulgated by the Pope in 1870. It is difficult to gain access, but in any case its most striking feature is the superb portal of the entrance, a noble Renaissance work dating to 1520.

Wipplingerstrasse 6. Trams 1 and 2 to Börse.

SCHOTTENKIRCHE (Church of the 'Scottish' Monks)

In 1155, the Babenberg Duke Heinrich II invited Benedictine monks to found a monastery here. They actually came from Ireland, not Scotland. A privilege of the monastery was the immunity from judgement granted to those on the run who managed reach its precincts (hence the name *Freyung* for the square). The church was substantially rebuilt in the 19th century and is not one of Vienna's most beautiful.

However (currently) in the Chapter House is its greatest treasure from the Gothic period, the Schottenaltar (1475), with panels containing the earliest views of Vienna.

Freyung. Access to the Chapter House only on Saturdays at 2pm. From 1993 the Schottenaltar will be placed in its own museum in the former prelacy. The church will be temporarily closed during building works. Trams 1 and 2, U2 to Schottentor.

DONNER BRUNNEN (Donner Fountain)

The fountain is so called after the sculptor Georg Raphael Donner, who made it in 1739. The central seated figure is 'Providence' and around her are personifications of the rivers bordering on Lower Austria. Their nakedness shocked Maria Theresa, who had the fountain removed in 1773. It is now in the Lower Belvedere – this is a copy.
Neuer Markt. U1 and U3 to Stephansplatz.

DOROTHEUM

Joseph I founded a state pawnbroker in 1707 to curb the rampant exploitation in the pawn trade. The institution got its name when it moved into the convent of the Dorothean nuns, dissolved by Joseph II. The present interior is neo-baroque or later. Furniture and *objets d'art* are regularly auctioned under state auspices and anyone may view the goods or attend auctions.
Dorotheergasse 17. Trams 1 and 2, U1, U2, U4 to Karlsplatz/Oper.

FERSTEL PALAIS (Ferstel Palace)

Many consider the Ferstel Palais to be the finest example of romantic historicism in Vienna. Heinrich Ferstel was commissioned to design a multi-functional building to house the Austro-Hungarian Bank, the Stock Exchange, shops and a café; it also had to fit an irregularly shaped site.

His vivid and sumptuous building (1860), which draws inspiration from the Venetian and Florentine Renaissance, triumphantly solved these problems. An arcade runs through the middle of the building; in an inner light well is the Donaunixen–Brunnen (Fountain of the Danube Nymphs). The once famous literary haunt Café Central, frequented by such intellectuals as Sigmund Freud and Leon Trotsky, still occupies part of the ground floor (see page 24).
Freyung 2, Herrengasse 14. U3 to Herrengasse.

Works of art are put on display prior to auction at the Dorotheum

Old and new: Stephansdom and the controversial Haas Haus

GRABEN

The Graben, or ditch, was originally the outer fortification for the Roman camp. Later it was a market, before being built in with patrician houses. Its present aspect is mostly 19th century (for example the heavy historicist Grabenhof, nos 14–15). At no 21 the First Austrian Bank occupies a fine neoclassical building by Alois Pichl (1836). It is flanked by expensive shops (see pages 27 and 94).
Graben. U1 and U3 to Stephansplatz.

HAAS HAUS (Haas House)

Vienna's most spectacular and controversial recent piece of architecture by Hans Hollein, opened in 1990. From the top floor a good view of St Stephen's may be had from the convex-windowed café (see page 27).
Stock-im-Eisen-Platz 6. U1 and U3 to Stephansplatz.

HEILIGENKREUZER HOF (Holy Cross Court)

In the 17th century Abbott Schäffer of the Cistercian Abbey at Heiligenkreuz had the present baroque buildings constructed, incorporating earlier Gothic parts. The St Bernard chapel contains fine work by the painters Martin Altomonte and Antonio Tassi and the sculptor Giovanni Giuliani, dating to the 18th century (see page 29).
Schönlaterngasse 5 and Grashofgasse 3. U1 and U3 to Stephansplatz.

HOFKAMMERARCHIV (Imperial Archives)

The Imperial Archive contains the documents relating to the administration of the Habsburgs' realms. The playwright Franz Grillparzer, who was employed as head of the archive, worked here and his room is preserved as a memorial.
Apply to the porter or tel: 512 54 34. Johannesgasse 6. U1 and U3 to Stephansplatz.

MARIA THERESA'S CHASTITY COMMISSION

Distressed by the shameless philandering of her husband, Franz-Stephan, Maria Theresa decided to tackle the problem by making life difficult for paramours generally in her capital. Accordingly, in 1747 she set up her famous (or infamous) Chastity Commission, whose officials were empowered to pry into the houses of citizens if they had any reason to suspect that women of loose morals were on the premises. Singers, dancers and actresses were deemed to fall automatically into this category and, needless to say, no sanctions against men were envisaged. The Commission, says Edward Crankshaw in his biography of Maria Theresa, was received 'at first with incredulity, then with outrage, then with ridicule by the populace at large' and caused great amusement among foreigners.

HISTORISCHES MUSEUM DER STADT WIEN (Historical Museum of the City of Vienna)

The idea of a historical museum of the city was a natural concomitant to the romantic historicism of late-19th-century Vienna. Its first home was in the freshly built gothic City Hall, where it was opened in 1887. There were many plans to give the museum its own building, including one by Otto Wagner in 1903. It is to be regretted that this failed to be accepted, in view of the structure finally agreed upon in the late 1950s.

The contents of the museum are a different matter, offering a panoramic display of Viennese history on three floors. They cover the fields of topography, history, art and culture and benefit very considerably from this rounded concept of 'history'. The collection of pictures is worth seeing in itself, and includes works by leading baroque artists (Maulbertsch, Troger, Altomonte, Rottmayr), artists from the Biedermeier period (Amerling, Fendi, Danhauser) and the turn of the century (Klimt, Schiele, Kokoschka).

The **Ground Floor** deals with the prehistory of Vienna beginning with the Hallstatt period, and covering the Roman settlement and the Middle Ages up to the Renaissance.

The **First Floor** follows on chronologically with the baroque. There are portraits of Maria Theresa, her son, the dogmatically enlightened Emperor Joseph II, her husband Franz Stephan and her father Charles VI. Especially striking is the anonymous portrait of

Painting of a young woman by Waldmüller

Kara Mustafa, the unsuccessful Turkish grand vizier who laid siege to Vienna in 1683 and who was executed by the Sultan's emissaries by strangulation with a silk cord when he failed.

Of topographical interest is Augustin Hirschvogel's circular *Plan of Vienna* made in 1548. It may be compared with the elaborate *maquette* of the Inner City three centuries later by Eduard Fischer. There are other plans and bird's-eye views that repay study, together with engravings of street scenes and city life. Mozart lovers will be interested in the 1790 painting of a Freemasons' Lodge featuring both the composer and his librettist for *The Magic Flute*, Emanuel Schikaneder.

On the **Second Floor** one section deals with the Biedermeier Age (1815-1848), the period between the Congress of Vienna and the Revolution of 1848. The Revolution is well documented with objects and pictures. The reconstructed room from the home of the playwright Franz Grillparzer gives a good impression of a Biedermeier interior, where unpretentious elegance was the guiding principle.

An even more fascinating interior is that designed by the architect Adolf Loos for his own apartment at Bösendorferstrasse 3, where English influence is evident. From the same turn-of-the-century period come masterworks by Gustav Klimt, the leader of the Viennese Secession, (*Portraits of Emilie Flöge, Pallas Athene* and *Love*). There are also objects made by the leading Secessionist designers, Josef Hoffmann and Kolo Moser. Important cultural figures are represented sculpturally: for example Robert Musil, author of a great panoramic philosophical novel set in the dying days

Sixteenth-century suit of armour

of the Austro-Hungarian Empire, is portrayed in a bust by Fritz Wotruba; the writer Karl Kraus and the composer Anton Webern are featured in busts by Josef Humplik.

From Celtic fort to UNO-City, the stones, the artefacts, the people of Vienna come alive and speak with their individual voices here. It makes sense to devote a couple of hours to the museum at the beginning of your visit, and perhaps return at the end (see page 35). *Karlsplatz 8. Tel: 505 87 47. Open: Tuesday to Sunday 9am–4.30pm. Admission charge. Trams 1 and 2, U1, U2, U4 to Karlsplatz/Oper.*

The
Habsburgs
and their
Legacy

A tenacious and pious dynasty, with many adept or stoical survivors among its scions, the Habsburgs ruled a large part of Central Europe from Vienna for 640 years. The penultimate Emperor, Francis Joseph, reigned a record-breaking 68 years from the Revolution of 1848 to the middle of World War I. For centuries, Habsburgs were also elected Holy Roman Emperor, (although it was often necessary to bribe the Electors first).

In Vienna, they are remembered for their great monuments – the Hofburg (occupying 20 hectares and comprising some 2,500 rooms), the Palace of Schönbrunn (1,441 rooms), St Stephen's (whose great tower was begun under Rudolf IV), St Peter's (rebuilt on the initiative of Leopold I) and St Charles'

(Charles VI's homage for delivery from the plague).

The legacy of 'imperial and royal' Vienna lives on in the atmosphere of the city, as in its fabric. Francis Joseph's favourite dish of boiled beef (*Tafelspitz*) is on the menu of any typically Viennese restaurant. Traditional confectioners trade on their 'By Appointment' credentials. *Kaiserkitsch* – postcards or figurines of the aged Emperor Francis Joseph – abound in the souvenir shops. The myriad titles of the imperial bureaucracy are tenaciously clung to in a Republic where other titles are forbidden. Vienna will never be free of the Habsburgs and the Habsburg myth; but then, it does not wish to be.

Stephansdom's tower was begun during Rudolf IV's reign

Emperor Joseph one of the ny statues memorating Habsburgs

Emperor Francis Joseph, the longest reigning Habsburg

The Kaiserkrone in the Hofburg

The Palace of Schönbrunn: a great architectural monument

The Hofburg

*T*he later Babenberg Dukes moved from their palace 'Am Hof' to a site now under the complex of the Hofburg, and erected a new fortification, later occupied by the Bohemian King Ottokar Premysl (1251-1278). After Rudolf I of Habsburg defeated Ottokar in 1278, he too moved into the existing fortress. The Habsburgs based themselves here for six centuries, continually adding to the Gothic core in contemporary styles.

The last addition, the bombastic Neue Burg, was only completed in 1917, a year before the collapse of the Austro-Hungarian Empire. The oldest (Gothic) part of the Burg corresponded to the Schweizerhof and is preserved in the earlier sections of the Burgkapelle (Chapel) in its southeast corner. The chapel was much altered in the 15th century and the current appearance of the Schweizerhof dates to the 16th century. The Stallburg was built in the Renaissance, together with the Amalienburg (subsequently altered).

KAISERAPPARTEMENTS
(Imperial Apartments)

The apartments are (largely) preserved as Francis Joseph had them. The tour includes the rooms of his wife, Elisabeth, of the Bavarian ruling house of Wittelsbach and the rooms occupied by Tsar Alexander during the Congress of Vienna. Elisabeth's 'keep fit' appliances are a curiosity. The Banqueting Hall is laid out for a ceremonial dinner.

SCHATZKAMMER (Treasury)

The highlight is the Insignia and Regalia of the Holy Roman Empire, of which the Imperial Crown (Kaiserliche Hauskrone) dates to 962, probably made for the coronation of Otto the Great in Rome. There are also swords, crosses and reliquaries. Notable is the crown of Rudolph II made in Prague in 1602.

BURGKAPELLE (Hofburg Chapel)

The chapel was constructed under Friedrich III between 1447 and 1449. However, much of the original Gothic architecture has been obscured by subsequent alteration and the interior fittings are baroque. From the 17th century the Hofmusikkapelle (Court Music Chapel), as it is called, became important; among its directors was Johann Joseph Fux (1715-40), the leading music teacher of his day. Salieri, Gluck, Mozart, and Bruckner all performed here in the course of their careers. The Vienna Boys Choir sings mass on Sundays at 9.15am (also on festivals) from mid-September to late June. Tickets in advance from the chapel on the preceding Friday, or from agencies, or on the day if any are left.

SCHWEIZERTOR (Swiss Gate)

The 'Swiss' appellation is a reference to the fact that under Maria Theresa Swiss guards were employed in the Burg. The splendid Renaissance gateway was designed (probably) by Pietro Ferrabosco in 1553; the inscription in Latin lists the titles of Ferdinand I, Emperor at the time.

THE HOFBURG

With some justification the Hofburg has been described as a city within a city: the vast complex of buildings begun in the 13th century now has 18 wings, 54 stairways and some 2,600 room. There are 19 courtyards within or around the buildings; 110 of the apartments are lived in, while 45 are used as offices. Then, of course, there are the cellars and gardens. Around 5,000 people live or work in the Hofburg.

Between Schweizerhof and In der Burg.
Standing with your back to the Schweizertor, In der Burg, the baroque Leopoldinischer Trakt (now the office of the Federal President) is on your left (built under Leopold I), the Amalienburg (named after the widow of Joseph I) straight ahead, the Reichskanzleitrakt (for administration of the Holy Roman Empire) and the Michaelertrakt on your right.
Hofburg: trams 1 and 2 to Burgring.
Kaiserappartements: entry under the cupola of the Michaelertor. Open: Monday to Saturday 8.30am–noon, 12.30pm – 4pm; Sunday/bank holidays 8.30am–12.30pm. Admission charge.
Opposite is the Imperial Tableware and Silver Treasury. Tel: 533 10 44. Open:
Tuesday to Friday and Sunday 9am–1pm. Admission charge.
Schatzkammer: on the south side of the Schweizerhof. Tel: 533 60 46. Open: Wednesday to Monday 10am-6pm. Admission charge.
Burgkapelle: entrance above the entrance of the Treasury. Tel: 533 99 27, 533 50 67.

NATIONALBIBLIOTHEK
(National Library)

The commission for the superb former Court Library was given to Johann Bernhard Fischer von Erlach by Charles VI. It was to house the library of the Habsburgs, to which that of Prince Eugene of Savoy was later added. Although Fischer von Erlach the Elder did the designs, it was his son Joseph Emanuel who carried the project through to completion in 1735. The interior is generally considered the finest of any library in the world, with splendid Corinthian columns and pilasters flanking the Prunksaal (Hall of State), which has a high oval cupola. The fresco in the cupola represents the apotheosis of Charles VI by Daniel Gran. The marble statue of the emperor in the centre, and those of other personages at each end, are by Paul and Peter von Strudel.

Fiakers line up outside the Hofburg

WINTERREITSCHULE (Winter Riding School)

On the northwest side of the Josefsplatz is the Redoute, originally used for theatrical performances, then as ballrooms, where delegates to the Congress of Vienna waltzed the night away, provoking the Prince de Ligne's celebrated remark: *'Le congrès danse, mais il ne marche pas'* (the congress dances but does nothing).

Adjoining it is the Winter Riding School, designed by Fischer von Erlach the Younger, where the famous Lipizzaners perform their unique combination of dressage and ballet. At the north end is the Emperor's box with a large equestrian portrait of Charles VI by Johann Georg Hamilton and Gottfried Auerbach. The riders doff their hats to this before starting work. Booking for performances is from the

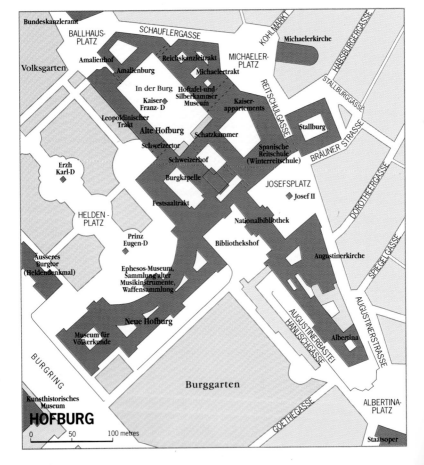

Bundeskanzleramt
BALLHAUS-PLATZ
SCHAUFLERGASSE
KOHLMARKT
Michaelerkirche
HABSBURGERGASSE
Amalienhof
Reichskanzleitrakt
MICHAELER-PLATZ
Volksgarten
Amalienburg
Michaelertrakt
STALLBURGGASSE
In der Burg
Hoftafel-und Silberkammer Museum
Kaiser-appartements
REITSCHULGASSE
Kaiser-Franz-D
Leopoldinischer Trakt
Stallburg
Alte Hofburg
Schatzkammer
Spanische Reitschule (Winterreitschule)
BRÄUNER STRASSE
Schweizertor
Schweizerhof
Erzh Karl-D
Burgkapelle
JOSEFSPLATZ
DOROTHEERGASSE
Festsaaltrakt
Josef II
HELDEN-PLATZ
Nationalbibliothek
Prinz Eugen-D
Bibliothekshof
Ausseres Burgtor (Heldendenkmal)
Ephesos-Museum, Sammlung alter Musikinstrumente, Waffensammlung
Augustinerkirche
SPIEGELGASSE
Neue Hofburg
AUGUSTINERBASTEI
HANUSCHGASSE
AUGUSTINERSTRASSE
Museum für Völkerkunde
Albertina
BURGRING
Burggarten
Kunsthistorisches Museum
ALBERTINA-PLATZ
HOFBURG
0   50   100 metres
GOETHEGASSE
Staatsoper

office under the cupola of the Michaelertor. Some tickets are also available in travel agencies. Since performances are often booked out you may have to settle for a 'morning training' session.

STALLBURG (Imperial Stables)

After a serious outbreak of disease among the horses a few years ago, visits to the stables have come to an end. The triple-storeyed Renaissance building with its lovely arcades was originally built for Archduke (later Emperor) Maximilian in 1558.

NEUE BURG

On the east side of the Heldenplatz is the vast colonnaded façade of the semi-circular Neue Burg. In Gottfried Semper's original plan for an 'Imperial Forum', a similar semicircle would have faced it from the other side of the square, and both would have been linked across the Ringstrasse to the Museum of Natural History and the Museum of Art History.

However, Emporor Francis Joseph only approved the plans for the new wing of the palace. Various architects worked on the Neue Burg, which was completed only in 1917. It now houses the main reading rooms of the National Library, the Weapons Collection and Collection of Old Musical Instruments of the Museum of Art History, together with the Museum of Ethnology and the Ephesus Museum.

HELDENPLATZ (Heroes Square)

Facing each other on the square are the two massive equestrian statues of Prince Eugene of Savoy and Archduke Carl, respectively heroes of the Turkish and the Napoleonic Wars. The Heldenplatz,

originally a parade-ground, is one of the focal points of the city; from the balcony of the Neue Burg Hitler ranted at the hysterically cheering crowds in 1938 after the Anschluss (annexation) of Austria with Germany. On the southwest side is the Burgtor, giving egress to the Ringstrasse. It was erected by Franz I in memory of the Battle of the Nations at Leipzig, where Napoleon was defeated.

Nationalbibliotek: entrance from Josefsplatz 1. Prunksaal (tel: 534 10-397). Open: Monday to Saturday 10am–4pm, Sunday and holidays 10am–1pm. Late opening Tuesday 7.45pm. October to May, Monday to Saturday 11am–noon. The Globenmuseum (Museum of Maps and Globes) is in the same building (tel: 534 10/297). Open: Monday to Wednesday and Friday 11am–noon, Thursday 2pm–3pm.
Winterreitschule: entrance Josefsplatz Door 3. Morning training (usually Tuesday to Saturday 10am–noon).
Stallburg: entrance from Augustiner-strasse.
Neue Burg: entrance from Heldenplatz. Opening times:
Ephesus Museum – Wednesday to Monday 10am–4pm. Musical Instruments – Wednesday to Monday 10am–6pm. Weapons Collection – presently under reconstruction.
Ethnological Museum – Monday, Thursday to Saturday 10am–1pm, Wednesday 10am–5pm, Sunday 9am–1pm.
Admission charges.
Central tel: 93 45 41.
Opening hours of the National Library (Reader's ticket required): September to July, Monday to Friday 2am–7.45pm, Saturday 9am–1pm; mid-July to end of August, Monday to Friday 9am–3.45pm, Saturday 9 am–1pm.
Library tel: 534 10-397.

Lipizzaners

The lovely white Lipizzaners that perform in the Spanish Riding School (so-called because originally only horses of Spanish origin were employed) represent the perfection of breeding and training. The breed, with Spanish, Neapolitan and Arab antecedents, takes its name from the stud at Lipica (now in Slovenia) established in 1580 by the Archduke Karl. The horses are born dark, only acquiring their distinctive white sheen around the age of seven.

The performances in the school demonstrate the principles of *haute école*, a demanding routine of exercises carried out above the ground as well as on it, and requiring absolute discipline, versatility and sensitivity from the horses and their riders. Feats like the famous *Capriole* in the air, or *Levade* on the hindlegs, have their origin in cavalry techniques, but were subsequently refined and stylised to produce something akin to a horse ballet (the exercises are to music and end with a School Quadrille). It is a tradition, uniquely preserved in Vienna, a glimpse of the baroque age frozen in a time-warp.

The riding displays are a joy to watch

The Viennese are rightly proud of the Spanish Riding School

The horses follow a four-year training programme

WIEN.
PORZELLANMANUFAKTUR
AUGARTEN
Wien 2, Schloss-Augarten
Wien 1, Stock-im-Eisen-Platz 3
Wien 6, Mariahilferstrasse 99
Linz-Donau, Rainerstrasse 20
Salzburg, Schwarzstrasse 18
Graz, Hauptplatz 5

The extraordinary skill of the Lipizzaner horses

HUNDERTWASSERHAUS

The painter Friedensreich Hundertwasser created this multi-coloured apartment block in 1985, commissioned by the city council. A committed 'green', he reduced synthetic materials to a minimum and employed brick and wood as much as possible. It defies all rules of conventional architecture and is well worth a visit.
Corner of Kegelgasse and Löwengasse. Tram N from Schwedenplatz.

JOSEPHINUM

The Josephinum was originally an institution for the training of military doctors (it takes its name from Emperor Joseph II, who commissioned the building). The architect of this, one of the finest pieces of Josephin neoclassical architecture in Vienna, was Isidor Canevale, who completed it in 1785. However, apart from the fine library, its main interest to visitors is the extra-ordinary collection of 1,192 anatomical wax models made in Florence to the specifications of Felice Fontana and Paolo Mascagni (see page 37).
Währinger Strasse 25. Tel: 43 12 54. Open: Monday to Friday 9am–3pm. Admission charge. Trams 38, 40, 41 and 42 – in walking distance of Schottentor.

Modern shopping in Kärntner Strasse

KARLSKIRCHE (Church of St Charles Borromeo)

After the plague of 1713 had claimed more than 8,000 victims in Vienna, the Emperor Charles VI decided to build a church to the saint who protected against the disease, St Charles Borromeo of Milan. A competition for the design was won by Johann Bernhard Fischer von Erlach against the greatest architects of the day (including Hildebrandt and Galli-Bibiena). His plans were completed after his death by his son Joseph Emanuel. The Church of St Charles is the greatest baroque masterwork of the city, some say of Europe. It boasts a massive copper dome surmounting lateral pavilions and has a broad antique portico. Antiquity is again recalled in the great columns that stand before the church – inspired by Trajan's column in Rome – which show the life of St Charles in an ascendant spiralling frieze. The interior contains frescos by Johann Michael Rottmayr and paintings by leading baroque artists – Daniel Gran, Sebastiano Ricci and others (see page 35).
Karlsplatz. Trams 1 and 2, U1, U2, U4 to Karlsplatz/Oper.

KÄRNTNER STRASSE (Carinthia Street)

This ancient thoroughfare takes its name from the old trading route to the south that entered the city through the 'Carinthian' Gate (adjacent to where the Opera now stands) and ran through to St Stephen's, as the street still does. It bore the name Carinthia Street as early as 1257. Kärntner Strasse has fallen victim to ugly architectural renewal since World War II, but the diminutive Gothic Church of the Knights of St John of Malta still stands at no 37, together with

Henry Moore's sculpture contrasts with the baroque Karlskirche

the attractive Palais Esterházy at no 51. However, the street will be remembered by most visitors as the most seductive of Vienna's shopping malls.
Trams 1 and 2, U1, U2 and U4 to Karlsplatz/Oper, or U1 and U3 to Stephansplatz.

KIRCHE AM STEINHOF (Steinhof Church)

On a hill in the 14th district stands the complex of buildings comprising Vienna's psychiatric hospital. At the highest point of it one of the most

remarkable buildings by the Secessionist architect, Otto Wagner, was constructed in 1907. Although the exterior is certainly striking, it is the interior that has fascinated architectural specialists and laymen alike. The gilded inside of the dome (which is artificially divided from the exterior) produces an effect like stars, in the middle of which a cross seems to float. The benches are rounded at the edges to prevent patients injuring themselves and there are other hygienic features such as running water in the stoop.
Baumgartner Höhe 1. Bus 48A. Visits of the interior may only be in groups, usually only on Saturday afternoons.

Kunsthistorisches Museum

(Museum of Art History)

When Francis Joseph ordered the opening up of Vienna in 1857 through the demolition of the old city's bastions and the erection of public and private buildings, there were soon ambitious plans for the city's expansion. One of these was Gottfried Semper's project for an 'Imperial Forum' which would include new museums for the vast but scattered Habsburg collections. The Museum of Art History, and the

The Kunsthistorisches Museum

Museum of Natural History facing it across Maria-Theresien-Platz are what remain of these grand designs. The museums were begun by Semper and Karl Hasenauer together, and ended by Hasenauer on his own after the two quarrelled. Their ceremonial opening took place in 1891.

The great stairway leading up to the galleries of the Museum of Art History is itself a work of art, with lunettes painted by Hans Makart, the brothers Ernst and Gustav Klimt and Franz Matsch. The ceiling frescos are by the Hungarian Mihály Munkácsy and represent *The Apotheosis of the Renaissance*. On the landing is Antonio Canova's sculpture of *Theseus and the Centaur,* moved here from the Theseion in the Volksgarten (see pages 22, 117 and 122).

The collection of the Kunsthistorisches Museum is scattered – Musical Instruments, Arms and Armour and Ephesus Excavations are in the Neue Burg, while Crown Jewels and Ecclesiastical Treasures are in the Old Burg (see pages 68 71) and Coaches and Carriages are at Schönbrunn (see pages 104–7). In the building at Burgring 5 are the main collections of paintings, sculpture, decorative art and coins and medals.

On the **Ground Floor** are to be found Egyptian antiquities, Greek and Roman sculpture, Paleo-Christian art, decorative art, clocks and automata, and

A spacious exhibition of exellent works

Burgring 5. Entry from Maria-Theresien-Platz. Tel: 93 45 41. Opening times for the Kunsthistorisches Museum: Tuesday to Sunday 10am–6pm. Picture Gallery only open Tuesday and Friday 7pm–9pm (March to October from 6pm). Admission charge. Trams 1 and 2 to Burgring.

The perfect setting for fine art

Renaissance and Mannerist work. Those looking for Benvenuto Cellini's famous gold salt-cellar (1543) will find it in Room XXVII.

On the **First Floor** is the picture gallery, among the richest in the world, and the fourth largest. It represents assiduous collection by the Habsburgs from the 17th century onwards and naturally is most representative of the art of those lands over which they had supremacy at one time or another. This means that Dutch and Venetian painting are specially prominent, but there are also German, French and English masters in the collection. The Spanish part is modest in size but high in quality; child portraits of the Spanish Princess Margarita Teresa by Velázquez were sent for inspection to Vienna during the long marriage negotiations between the two dynastic branches – eventually she was married to Leopold I (see Cabinet 10).

Perhaps the most celebrated pictures in the whole museum are the Brueghels, of which the representation is probably the best in the world (Room X). Other Dutch artists well represented are Van Dyck, Rubens and Rembrandt; of the Germans, Cranach, Dürer, and Holbein. An entire room (II) is devoted to Titian.

On the **Second Floor** are townscapes by Bernardo Bellotto, nephew of Canaletto, they show 18th-century Vienna, including the Belvedere, Freyung, the Dominican Church and Schönbrunn. On the same floor is the Coins and Medals Collection, 4,500 being on display out of some 500,000 items (see page 34).

MUSEUM DES 20 JAHR–HUNDERTS (Museum of the 20th Century)

The design for this modest shrine of contemporary art was originally that for the Austrian pavilion at the Brussels World Exhibition of 1958. The architect was Karl Schwanzer. The glass panels of the ground floor look out on to a sculpture garden. The museum, which is actually an offshoot of the Museum of Modern Art (see below) has a small permanent collection of sculptures, including works by Arp, Giacometti, Moore and Rodin. However, its main function is to put on a rolling programme of shows devoted to modern artists or themes (see page 31).
Schweizer Garten. Tel: 78 25 50. Open: Thursday to Tuesday 10am–6pm. Admission charge. Tram D from Schwarzenbergplatz.

The Museum of Modern Art

MUSEUM MODERNER KUNST IM PALAIS LIECHTENSTEIN (Museum of Modern Art in the Liechtenstein Palace)

The Museum of Modern Art (Ludwig Foundation) is housed rather incongruously in the fine baroque palace built for the Liechtensteins by D E Rossi and Domenico Martinelli (see page 37). If current plans come to fruition, the Museum of Modern Art and its appendage in the Schweizer Garten will be incorporated in the great exhibition centre planned for the Messepalast (former Imperial Stables). Among the more interesting items in the collection are works by Austrian Expressionists, in particular Max Oppenheimer and Richard Gerstl. Egon Schiele's extremely powerful *Portrait of Eduard Kosmack* is also here and there is painting by Oskar Kokoschka. Works by non-Austrians include those by Ferdinand Léger, Max Ernst, René Magritte and Ben

Nicholson. Near the entrance is a sculpture by Fritz Wotruba, architect of the extraordinary Wotruba Church in the suburb of Mauer (see page 119). *Fürstengasse 1. Tel: 34 12 59. Open: Wednesday to Monday 10am–6pm. Admission charge. Tram D from Schottentor.*

ÖSTERREICHISCHES MUSEUM FÜR ANGEWANDTE KUNST (Austrian Museum of Applied Arts)

A professor for History of Art at the Vienna University visited the World Exhibition in London in 1862 and was so impressed with the South Kensington Museum (now the Victoria and Albert Museum) that he immediately set about founding an Austrian museum for art and industry on his return. His agitation was successful and the government appointed Heinrich Ferstel to design the new museum. Any design had to take into account the School of Applied Art which was attached to the whole. The building that was completed in 1871 is in the style of the Italian High Renaissance, and looks particularly striking since its complete restoration (1990–92). Ferstel insisted on using only the highest quality materials in his buildings, a fact that is evident from both the external and internal aspects of the museum. The great vestibule that you step into is surrounded by graceful arcades on the Ground and First Floor, and was inspired by the Palazzo Vecchio in Florence.

The **Ground Floor** rooms are devoted to furniture and *objets d'art*, and in the extensions are artefacts of Islam and the Orient, including carpets, Chinese bronzes, T'ang porcelain, glass and ceramics. Also on the ground floor, in the section devoted to 17th- and 18th-

The Academy of Applied Arts

century Europe, is a fine representation of Meissen ware.

On the **First Floor** there is much of more specifically Austrian interest particularly in the section devoted to the Biedermeier period, glass, Augarten porcelain, and a collection of stoves. The Jugendstil (Art Nouveau) furniture includes pieces designed by Josef Hoffmann, Kolo Moser and others. *Stubenring 5. Tel: 711 36–0. Recorded information: 712 80 00. The museum is scheduled to re-open in 1992 after extensive renovation. Open: Wednesday to Monday 11am–6pm. Admission charge. Trams 1 and 2 to Dr-Karl-Lueger-Platz, U3 to Stubentor.*

Furniture enthusiasts may also be interested in the Bundesmobiliendepot (Court Furniture Repository). *Mariahilfer Strasse 88. Tel: 523 42 40. Guided tours on the hour: Tuesday to Friday 9am–4pm, Saturday 9am–noon). Admission charge.*

Smaller and Unusual Museums

There is a museum in Vienna catering to almost every conceivable taste. Josef Schwingsmehl, the proprietor of a Sex Museum in the Prater, boasts that it is the only one of its kind in the world (Strasse des 1 Mai, open: daily noon–11.30pm), and similar claims could be made for some other collections. The following is a selection of some of the more interesting or bizarre offerings.

Exquisite panelling on carriage door

BESTATTUNGSMUSEUM (Burial Museum)

The Viennese reputation for the enjoyment of sensual pleasures is only equalled by their fascination with death and all its trappings. The Burial Museum documents Viennese burial rites and offers some fascinating glimpses of past attitudes and practices. There is even a coffin with an 'emergency cord' to the surface for those wrongly pronounced dead, who come to their senses only to discover they have already been buried.
Goldeggasse 19. Tel: 501 95/227. Open: Monday to Friday noon–3pm, by telephone appointment. Admission charge.

FIAKER MUSEUM (Hackney Coach Museum)

The name of the 'Fiaker' comes from the French fiacre, so-called because they lined up in front of the St Fiacre Church in Paris. Nowadays fiakers are exclusively for sight-seeing, around 30 of them operating from Heldenplatz and Stephansplatz. The museum documents the history of the fiaker in Vienna.
Veronikagasse 12. U6 to Josefstädter Strasse. Tel: 43 26 07. Open: every first Wednesday in the month 10am–1pm. Admission charge.

KRIMINALMUSEUM (Crime Museum)

Vienna's newest museum (opened in 1991) offers an array of criminality for the ghoulish, the concerned and the buffs.
Grosse Sperlgasse 24. Open: daily except Monday 10am–5pm. Admission charge. Tram N.

MUSEUM DER MECHIT-ARISTEN-KONGREGATION (Mechitharist Museum)

The Armenian Uniat congregation was founded by Mekhitar (1676–1749) in 1701 and was subsequently based in the

Veneto. This rather unusual collection offers an insight into Armenian culture and religious practice.
Mechitaristengasse 4. Tel: 93 64 17. Visits by prior appointment. Tram 46, Bus 48A.

THEATERMUSEUM (Theatre Museum)

Vienna is world-famous as a theatre city, both as a breeding ground of first class stage actors and as a place where comedian–playwright–actor–managers have thrived. The most famous of these created new genres of theatre and unforgettable stage personas: such were Anton Stranitzky (1676–1726), who invented the *Hanswurst* clown character, Ferdinand Raimund (1790–1846) and Johann Nestroy (1801–1862). In the late 19th century Alexander Girardi created typical stereotypes of Viennese characters which the Viennese themselves began to copy. 'We (Viennese) are always play-acting' remarked the writer Arthur Schnitzler; 'the wise man remembers that.'

The Theatre Museum offers a rich collection of photographs, costumes, players' texts, models for stage-sets and memorabilia.
Hanuschgasse 3 and Lobkowitzplatz 2. Individual shows put on by the Theatre Museum are now held in the nearby Lobkowitz Palais, the permanent exhibition in Hanuschgasse. Tel: 512 24 27; Palais Lobkowitz tel: 512 88 00. Open: Tuesday to Saturday 9am–12.30, 1.30pm–5pm. Sunday 9am–1pm. Admission charge. Trams 1 and 2, U1, U2, U4 to Karlsplatz/Oper.

UHRENMUSEUM (Clock Museum)

This wonderful collection of clocks was accumulated by its former curator

Time for the Uhrenmuseum

Rudolf Kaftan and the novelist Marie von Ebner-Eschenbach (1830–1916). It is located in the picturesque former Obizzi Palais, a building which dates back at least to the 16th century, although a house was on this site as early as the 11th century. The collection is so rich that it is invidious to pick out individual highlights from the 900 exhibits, that include all manner of pendant and pocket watches, mantel clocks, bracket clocks and travelling clocks. Particularly appealing are the naive picture clocks from the Biedermeier era (see page 25).
Schulhof 2, behind Am Hof. Tel: 533 22 65. Open: Tuesday to Sunday 9am–4.30pm. Admission charge. Trams 1 and 2 and U2 to Schottentor.

Mozart in Vienna

Wolfgang Amadeus Mozart came to Vienna in the entourage of the Prince-Archbishop of Salzburg, who treated him as a servant (he was seated at table just above the cooks), and forbade him to take on outside work. After a major row in 1781 he was literally booted out of the archbishop's employ – although the flunkey's boot also 'kicked open the door to the Viennese classical era'.

Mozart was self-willed, ambitious and not always prudent. To his father's horror he not only lost his job, but also married for love a spirited but ill-favoured daughter of a musician. Like Mozart, she had no idea how to handle money. Perhaps *The Abduction from the Seraglio* (whose heroine was called Constanze) was a sort of wedding present. Its première was two weeks before the ceremony in 1782, and was well received, although the Emperor complained that it had 'too many notes'.

Despite the initial success of, for example, *The Magic Flute*, now regarded as the quintessential Viennese opera, Mozart suffered from intrigues by Salieri and others and the whims of patrons. He got into debt and regularly had to borrow money from a fellow Freemason. Eventually he became ill while writing what he came to believe would be his own Requiem. On the 5th of December 1791 he died, and was unceremoniously buried in St Mark's Cemetery, the few mourners abandoning the coffin at the city gate because of the bitterly cold weather.

*A Mozart concert playe
period*

A statue of Mozart in the Burggarten

The Vienna Concert House: now a venue for works by the great composer

Music and Composers in Vienna

*M*usic is the life-blood of Vienna, as it has been for 200 years; however, the home-grown composers – such as Schubert and the Strauss dynasty – are outnumbered, if not outshone by the famous imports from elsewhere in Austrian lands (Mozart, Bruckner) or from abroad, chiefly Germany (Beethoven, Brahms, Richard Strauss and Mahler). The availability of patronage and a musically literate audience were perhaps two of the things that lured people to the Danubian metropolis, not forgetting the attractions of the city itself. Those who have contributed to the musical culture are remembered all over the city with monuments, statues and memorial rooms.

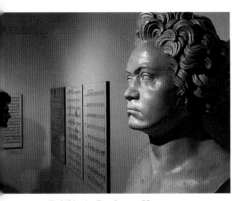

Exhibits in Beethoven Haus

LUDWIG VAN BEETHOVEN

Beethoven is said to have moved 80 times during his 36 years in Vienna, although he often returned to previously vacated rooms. This fidgeting was due partly to the composer's restless temperament, partly to the fact that not everyone tolerated his habits – playing the piano and 'singing' at all hours for instance, or forgetting to empty his chamber pot.

Eroica Haus

A memorial room recalls that the *Eroica* was written here, the dedication to Napoleon being torn out when the composer heard that the latter had had himself crowned Emperor.
Döblinger Hauptstrasse 92. Tel: 369 14 24. Open: Tuesday to Sunday 9am–12.15pm, 1pm–4.30pm. Tram 37.

Beethoven Haus

In a letter written to his brothers from this house in 1802 (subsequently known as the *Heiligenstädter Testament*) Beethoven movingly describes his feelings on realising that he was slowly going deaf – just as he was beginning to succeed as a composer (see page 39).
Probusgasse 6. Tel: 37 54 08. Open: Tuesday to Sunday 9am–12.15pm, 1pm–4.30pm. Buses 37A, 38A.

Pasqualati Haus

Beethoven lived here between 1804 and 1808, and again between 1810 and 1814, working on several of his symphonies, the violin concerto, and the final version

The house where Beethoven lived

of *Fidelio*. There are also memorial rooms to the novelist Adalbert Stifter.
Mölker Bastei 8. Tel: 637 06 65. Open: 9am–12.15pm, 1pm–4.30pm. Trams 1 and 2, U2 to Schottentor.

Beethoven Monument
The statue shows Beethoven seated, surrounded by allegorical allusions to the Ninth Symphony.
Beethovenplatz (behind Schubertring).

JOHANNES BRAHMS
Brahms Monument
An imposing seated statue of the cur-mudgeonly composer by Rudolf Weyr.
Resselpark (adjoining Karlsplatz).

ANTON BRUCKNER
Bruckner Monument
A copy of a bronze bust by Viktor Tilgner, which captures the character of the unworldly Anton Bruckner.
Stadtpark.

JOSEPH HAYDN
Haydn Museum
Haydn bought the house in 1793 and subsequently added to it. He wrote *The Creation* and *The Seasons* here. There is also a memorial room to Johannes Brahms.

Haydngasse 19 (south of Mariahilfer Strasse). Tel: 596 13 07. Open: Tuesday to Sunday 9am–12.15pm and 1pm–4.30pm. Trams 52, 58 to Westbahnhof.

LEHÁR-SCHIKANEDER-SCHLÖSSL
(Lehár-Schikaneder-Villa)
Various types of memorabilia relating to the astonishingly successful operetta composer, Franz Lehár, and the playwright and theatre manager Emanuel Schikaneder, are assembled here.
Hackofergasse 18. U4 to Heiligenstadt. Group visits only by prior appointment.

INSPIRATION IN THE AIR?
Born geniuses can probably compose anywhere and under any (or almost any) circumstances. Mozart's creative flow seemed largely unimpaired by intolerable distractions and pressures. It is hard to judge the exact impact of his surroundings on his music, although *The Magic Flute* neatly caught the Viennese aptitude for mixing the absurd with the profound. Schubert, on the other hand, seems exactly to express his Viennese milieu, its charm and grace with an underlying melancholy; Brahms claimed to work better in Vienna because of its village atmosphere. Only Beethoven, however, is on record as reproducing the effect of the surrounding countryside – that between Grinzing and Heiligenstadt – in the bird songs of the *Pastoral Symphony*; and also the mood inspired in him by Schönbrunn Park, in his overture to *Leonora* (the original title of *Fidelio*).

WOLFGANG AMADEUS MOZART

Compared to Beethoven, Mozart was a considerably more settled inhabitant of Vienna; yet even he moved three times during his 10-year sojourn in the city. His early lodgings were at Graben no 8: then he lived in the Domgasse no 5 and was eventually to die in the Rauhensteingasse no 8.

'Figaro' House

Mozart spent most of his time in Vienna in the very oldest part of the city around St Stephen's. In the 18th-century burgher house at no 5 Domgasse he lived between 1784 and 1787, a period often regarded as the happiest of his Vienna years. The name of the house refers to the fact that his sparkling opera *The Marriage of Figaro* was composed here, together with three piano concertos. The entrance to the Mozart memorial rooms is in the Domgasse.

The Mozart Monument in the Burggarten

> ### MOZART'S SALARY
> On the death of Christoph Willibald Gluck in 1787, Mozart was given his only official token of recognition at court when he was appointed to succeed Gluck as court composer - at only half the latter's salary, however. He is said to have remarked drily that the money was 'too much for what I do, too little for what I can do'.

Domgasse 5, Schulerstrasse 8. Tel: 513 62 94. Open: Tuesday to Sunday 9am–12.15pm and 1pm–4.30pm. U1 and U3 to Stephansplatz.

Mozart Monument

A competition was held on the centenary of Mozart's death to erect a suitably imposing monument to one who was now the city's favourite son, although it had not appeared quite like that during his lifetime. The winner of the competition, Eduard Hellmer, was mysteriously not awarded the commission, which went to Viktor Tilgner, a procedure that aroused almost as much controversy as the site chosen. The monument moved from Albertinaplatz to its present location in 1953.
Burggarten. Trams 1 and 2 to Burgring.

FRANZ SCHUBERT
Schubert's Geburtshaus
(Birthplace of Schubert)

Franz Schubert was born in this house on 31 January, 1797, but the family moved when he was four. The building was restored after World War II. There is now a small museum.
Nussdorfer Strasse 54. Tel: 345 99 24. Open: Tuesday to Sunday 9am–12.15pm and 1pm–4.30pm. Trams 37 and 38.

Schubert Monument

Schubert sits meditating, pencil in hand and staves spread out on his knee. The statue is by Karl Kundmann (1872).
Stadtpark. Trams 1 and 2.

Schubert's Sterbehaus
(The House where Schubert Died)

The room in which Schubert died may be visited.
Kettenbrückengasse 6. Tel: 573 90 72. Open: 9am–12.15pm, 1pm–4-30. U4 to Kettenbrückengasse.

JOHANN STRAUSS, Father and Son

The Strauss dynasty was founded by Johann Strauss Senior (1804–1849). Together with Joseph Lanner (1801–1843) he started the tradition of popular orchestras playing waltzes, marches and the like in the fashionable cafés and parks of Metternich's Vienna. Lanner and Strauss began as partners and ended as rivals. His son Johann Junior (1825–1899) was even more successful, although his father had advised him against going into the business. By the time he was 28 he had several orchestras comprising a total of 300 musicians under his control. It was he who composed the immortal waltzes thought of as typically Viennese – *Voices of Spring, Tales from the Vienna Woods* and the *Blue Danube*. Yet his father's marvellous *Radetzky March* is perhaps even more beloved, and traditionally closes the New Year's Day Concert in the Musikverein.

Johann-Strauss-Wohnung (Johann Strauss's House)

Johann Strauss Junior lived here at the height of his career. Here he composed his *Blue Danube* waltz in 1867. Its first performance was a spectacular flop, largely due to the idiotic text that dealt with the sad state of the country after its defeat by Prussia in 1866. It was first given a non-choral performance in Paris and went on to conquer the world.
Praterstrasse 54. Tel: 24 01 21. Open: Tuesday to Sunday 9am–12.15pm and 1pm– 4.30. U1 to Nestroyplatz.

Strauss-Lanner-Monument

The statue shows Johann Strauss Senior and Josef Lanner in relaxed pose.
Rathauspark near Stadiongasse. Trams 1 and 2.

The king of waltz plays on

Johann Strauss Monument

Perhaps Vienna's most famous landmark, it displays the waltz king, Johann Strauss Junior, wooing sweet sounds from his violin.
Stadtpark. Trams 1 and 2.

Invitation
to the
Waltz

January and February in Vienna! The ball season is in full swing. According to an old tradition, visiting political celebrities show themselves off from the loggia boxes of the opera, the interior of which has been cleared for waltzing. Outside, a rent-a-crowd of malcontents demonstrates for whatever cause is flavour of the month.

It is all a far cry from the heady champagne whirl of the 19th century, when the geniuses of the waltz – the Strauss dynasty and Joseph Lanner – entranced the Viennese and caused serious-minded musicians like Robert Schumann to grumble about the unrepentant levity of musical taste. Waltzes (then called Ländler after a village in Upper Austria) were known in the 18th century and

waltz themes can be found in the works of Mozart and Beethoven.

The Congress of Vienna made the dance fashionable – indeed, it became a craze. The German, Carl Maria von Weber, established the concert waltz form with his *Invitation to the Waltz* (1819). But it was Johann Strauss the Younger who made it synonymous with Viennese gaiety and decadence – the waltz, enthused Richard Wagner, had become 'even more potent than alcohol'. The *Blue Danube* (composed in 1867) became an unofficial alternative national anthem to Haydn's majestic official one. The critic Eduard Hanslick wrote, 'It says, more succinctly and more warmly than words, everything of a flattering nature that can be said about Vienna.'

DDS Johann Strauss: the boat restaurant that provides a waltz with your meal

Strauss gave Vienna the waltz and the dance goes on and on

The elegance of the waltz

Palais

*A*ll these palaces are in or on the edge of the Inner City, and within easy walking distance of U-Bahn stations, as indicated. The list is by no means complete, but the examples chosen represent some of the finest baroque profane architecture in Vienna; in some cases they have interesting historical associations.

BATTHYÁNY-PALAIS

The palace is built from a core building of 1695 enlarged by the incorporation of two neighbouring houses. The splendid portals are in the manner of Fischer von Erlach. The widow of the Hungarian Field Marshall, Count Batthyány, lived here, a lady renowned for her beauty and influence (see page 23).
Bankgasse 2, Herrengasse 19. U3 to Herrengasse.

DIETRICHSTEIN-PALAIS

Some seven palaces in Vienna are associated with the name of this powerful noble family. This is one of the most pleasing, a reworking of an older building carried out by Franz Hillebrand in 1755. The rococo portals encompass majestic wooden doors.
Minoritenplatz 3. U3 to Herrengasse.

ESTERHAZY-PALAIS

Built on the site of an ancient Babenberg palace, this was one of the many residences of the inestimably rich Esterhazies. In the palace chapel, Joseph Haydn was often obliged to supply the music during his 29-year-long service to the princes.
Wallnerstrasse 4. U3 to Herrengasse.

LIECHTENSTEINISCHES MAJORATSHAUS (Liechtenstein Entailed Palace)

The Liechtensteins' Palace

The previous owners to the Liechtensteins commissioned this palace from Domenico Martinelli in 1694, although it was actually constructed by two other Italian master-builders, Antonio Riva and Gabriele de Gabriele. The latter had his own ideas about the stairway and there was a violent quarrel

between him and the architect. The interior was lavishly decorated by other leading Italian masters, including sculptures by Giovanni Giuliani and stucco by Santino Bussi. It was very modern for its time, the lifts that functioned between all four floors (footman operated) being one of the wonders of the city. As the name implies, it became the main residence of the senior branch of the Liechtensteins in Vienna, they having acquired it when it was still being built (see page 23).
Bankgasse 9, Minoritenplatz 4. U3 to Herrengasse.

LOBKOWITZ-PALAIS

This lovely, freshly restored palace, with its creamy white façade and golden-varnished window frames, was originally built for the Dietrichsteins by Giovanni Pietro Tencala in 1687. (The façade was altered in 1710 by Fischer von Erlach the Elder.) In 1753 Prince Lobkowitz acquired the palace. A successor of his was a patron of Beethoven, who gave the première of his *Eroica* symphony to an invited audience here in 1804. During the Congress of Vienna the Lobkowitzes were famous for the lavishness of the balls they gave. Their palace now plays host to the individual exhibitions staged as part of the programme of the Theatre Museum (see pages 26 and 81).
Lobkowitzplatz 2. Trams 1 and 2, U1, U2, U4 to Karlsplatz/Oper .

NEUPAUER-BREUNER PALAIS

A rich entrepreneur named Neupauer originally had this sumptuous palace built, but had to sell it to the Breuner family in 1749 because of financial difficulties. Access is now possible for previews of Sotheby's auctions, since the palace is their Vienna base.

The Clock Museum at Obizzi Palais

Singerstrasse 16. U1 and U3 to Stephansplatz.

OBIZZI PALAIS

A house has stood on this site since the 11th century; it was originally known as the 'Harp House' because of its shape. In 1580 it came into the possession of the Starhembergs. Ernst Rüdiger, Count Starhemberg, the commander of the garrison during the Turkish siege of 1683, was the owner at that time, and it is said that lead cannon balls were forged in the open fireplaces of the palace. In 1690 the Obizzi family acquired it and added a storey. It now houses the Clock Museum (see pages 25 and 81).
Schulhof 2. Trams 1 and 2, U2 to Schottentor, U3 to Herrengasse.

*The Palace-Kinsky shows off Hildebrandt's
decorative talents to good effect*

PALAIS-HARRACH

The present magnificent palace, newly
restored, was built in 1702 to plans by
Domenico Martinelli. Originally it also
contained the family's important picture
collection which was then transferred to
Schloss Rohrau in Lower Austria in
1970. Its recent history has been
chequered: for a while it was in the
possession of the City Council; after
some controversial dealings it later came
into the possession of the Creditanstalt
Bank, who have invested huge sums in

general renovation (see page 24).
*Freyung 3. Trams 1 and 2, U2 to
Schottentor.*

PALAIS-KINSKY

The man who gave the commission for
this building was the formidable Count
Daun, a former commander of the City,
Imperial Counsellor, Viceroy of Naples,
and Regent of the Spanish Netherlands,
to name a few of his offices. In deliberate
competition with his near neighbour, the
Ban (Governor) of Croatia, who had had
a palace built for himself in the
Renngasse, Daun employed Lukas von
Hildebrandt in 1713 to design this

elegant narrow-fronted building, with its famously splendid ceremonial staircase. It came into possession of the Kinsky family in the 1780s (see page 24).
Freyung 4. Trams 1 and 2, U2 to Schottentor.

PALAIS -TRAUTSON

Another lovely palace by Johann Bernhard Fischer von Erlach, the Trautson palace was for long the headquarters of Maria Theresa's Hungarian Lifeguards. It now belongs to the Ministry of Justice.
Museumstrasse 7. Trams 1 and 2 to Dr-Karl-Renner-Ring, U2 to Volkstheater.

PRINCE EUGENE OF SAVOY'S WINTER PALAIS

The great aristocracy usually had a 'summer' or 'garden' palace outside the Inner City, and withdrew to their supposedly cosier 'winter' palace within the walls during the cold months. Both Fischer von Erlach the Elder and Lukas von Hildebrandt, the greatest architects of their day, worked on this imposing residence. It now belongs to the Finance Ministry and is periodically open to the public for exhibitions.
Himmelpfortgasse 8. U1 and U3 to Stephansplatz.

SCHÖNBORN-BATTHYÁNY PALAIS

This is generally considered to be Johann Bernhard Fischer von Erlach's finest palace just as the nearby Palais-Kinsky ranks among the greatest achievements of his rival Hildebrandt. While the latter's genius lay in the harmonious use of confined space, the former's work possesses a monumental and massive quality, horizontally emphasised. The façade is richly ornamented with,

among others, reliefs of the deeds of Hercules.
Renngasse 4. Trams 1 and 2, U2 to Schottentor.

SCHWARZENBERG-PALAIS

The plans for the palace were originally prepared by Lukas von Hildebrandt, but Fischer von Erlach the Elder took over the project after the court equerry to Charles VI, Prince Adam Schwarzenberg, acquired the palace in 1716. Fischer von Erlach the Younger subsequently worked on it, and was responsible for introducing the first operational steam-driven machine in Austria, pumping water to the fountains. The palace is still in Schwarzenberg hands and much of it has been turned into a luxury hotel and restaurant (see page 30).
Rennweg 2, Schwarzenbergplatz 9. Trams 1 and 2 to Schwarzenbergplatz.

UNGARISCHE BOTSCHAFT (Hungarian Embassy)

In the darkest days of Communist tyranny the Hungarians wanted to sell their finest Viennese inheritance from the days of the Austro-Hungarian Empire to raise much needed cash, but the plan foundered. The building consists of two baroque palaces knocked together by Franz Hillebrand in 1784: one of those had been built by Fischer von Erlach, altered by the architect of Schönbrunn, Nikolaus Pacassi, and was for a while the Hungarian Chancellery. Those able to infiltrate a reception will have the chance to admire the ceiling fresco in the ceremonial hall of Maria Theresa founding the Order of St Stephan, by Franz Anton Maulbertsch (see page 23).
Bankgasse 4-6. U3 to Herrengasse.

Patrician Houses

*T*he Inner City of Vienna (First District) is regulated in its entirety by the Office of Protection of Monuments, so that not only churches and palaces, but also more modest buildings of historic interest cannot be altered in any way without permission. In the latter category are a number of patrician houses which retain attractive architectural features. The following is a selection of those which might interest the visitor.

ANNAGASSE nos 8, 14 and 18

The whole of this street, which is now a pedestrian zone, has largely retained its baroque character. Old patrician houses were often given memorable or absurd names, a practice that goes back to the days before houses were numbered in the late 18th century. Number 18 is 'The House of the Blue Cannon Ball' and was built to a design by Lukas von Hildebrandt, as was no 8. 'The House of the Blue Carp' at no 14 dates to the 17th century.

Trams 1 and 2, U1, U2, U4 to Karlsplatz/Oper. For Annakirche see page 56.

BÄCKERSTRASSE nos 7 and 16

With the sharp increase in the population of Vienna towards the end of the Middle Ages (there were 60,000 inhabitants by the middle of the 15th century) concentrated building became a necessity. In the 16th century the wide Bäckerstrasse was divided with a row of houses down the middle, the rear side eventually becoming 'Sonnenfelsgasse' in 1862.

Bäckerstrasse 7 dates from the 16th century and is notable for its lovely Renaissance courtyard with arcades. There is remarkably little Renaissance architecture in Vienna, partly because money that might have been available for construction was swallowed up in building the elaborate Italian-designed fortifications against the Turkish menace.

Bäckerstrasse 16 is a baroque house from 1712. For many years a restaurant on the site served cheap food to the hungry students, using leftovers from the court.

Trams 1 and 2, U3 to Dr-Karl-Lueger-Platz/Stubentor.

JUDENPLATZ

The medieval Jewish ghetto existed in this part of town before the pogrom of 1421; it grew up immediately adjacent to the Babenberg palace 'Am Hof' (see page 25), since the Jews depended entirely on the ruler's protection in the Middle Ages, the populace, whipped up by the Church, being actively hostile.

At Judenplatz 2 is 'Great Jordan's House', built in the 15th century and taking its name from a rich burgher named Jörg Jordan. The relief on the wall shows the baptism of Christ in the River Jordan with a Latin inscription. Most guide-books try to give the impression that this is a 'Memorial' to the happenings of 1421, implying remorse. On the contrary, it is a rabid celebration of them.

Trams 1 and 2, U2 to Schottentor. No 2 Zum Grossen Jordan.

Tuchlauben, home to wealthy merchants

NAGLERGASSE

The majority of houses in this narrow curved street, that follows the course of the Roman camp's protective wall, are historic, some of their baroque façades concealing Renaissance or Gothic originals.

U3 to Herrengasse.

SCHÖNLATERNGASSE nos 7-7a, 9

A house on this site was documented as early as 1212 and is known as the Basilisk House, this fabled beast having once been discovered in its well. Number 9 is the Old Smithy, still an iron-worker's shop and now also a restaurant with a literary club attached.

U1 and U3 to Stephansplatz.

TUCHLAUBEN NO 5 HOCHHOLZERHOF (Hochholzer Court, also known as Long Cellar House)

In 1984 the body of this remarkable building had to be demolished, but the richly ornamented, long, curving baroque façade was preserved. It takes its name from a prosperous butcher who once owned it.

The BAWAG Bank now owns the premises and has taken advantage of the pedestrian zone of Tuchlauben (originally the homes of wealthy cloth merchants in the Middle Ages) to erect an open-air gallery of modern sculpture, continued inside the cashier's hall. There is also a pleasant café where you can take refreshment.

U1 and U3 to Stephansplatz.

PARLAMENT (Houses of Parliament)

The Parlament is architect Theophil Hansen's most heartfelt tribute to the values of classical Greece. It took 10 years to build between 1873 and 1883 and closely followed the model of antiquity. A massive statue of Pallas Athene, goddess of wisdom was later erected in front of the building (not inside it, according to Viennese wits, since that was the one place where no wisdom could be expected to be found). There are two Houses in the Parliament, the Bundesrat consisting of delegates from the Federal States, and the Nationalrat elected by universal suffrage for four years. Visits are allowed to parts of the interior from no 3 Karl–Renner–

Pallas Athene standing outside Parlament

Platz, when the Parlament is not in session on weekdays (see page 22). *Trams 1 and 2, U3 to Dr-Karl-Renner-Ring/Volkstheater. Tel: 40 110-211.*

PATHOLOGISCH-ANATOMISCHES MUSEUM (including NARRENTURM – 'Fools' Tower')

This celebrated cylindrical tower for confining lunatics dates to the time of Joseph II and is nicknamed *Guglhupf* by the Viennese after a similarly shaped pound-cake. It now houses a gruesome collection of medical horrors such as lungs eaten away by nicotine and the world's most comprehensive display of gall and kidney stones (see page 33). *Spitalgasse 2. Tel: 43 86 72. Open: Thursdays 8am–11am (closed on holidays and in August). Tram 5.*

PESTSÄULE (Dreifaltigkeitssäule – Plague Monument – officially Trinity Column)

In many a small town of the former Habsburg lands the main square boasts a florid baroque column commemorating deliverance from the plague. The most striking of all such must surely be the one on the Graben in Vienna, the model for all others. It was proposed by Emperor Leopold I in 1679, perhaps the worst year of plague in the city's history, when as many as 150,000 may have died. It was to be dedicated to the Holy Trinity and the 'Nine Choirs of Angels'. At first a wooden column was put up, at the dedication of which the fiery preacher, Abraham a Sancta Clara delivered one of his apocalyptic discourses. After the defeat of the Turkish siege, the Court Architect Ludovico Burnacini and Johann Bernhard Fischer von Erlach, (among others), were involved in the design of this wonderfully rich successor to the wooden original. An elaborate scheme of visual imagery presents the doctrine of the Trinity in the decoration of the column. At the column's base Leopold I is graphically depicted kneeling in thanksgiving. A pillar of swirling cloud encrusted with iconographical figures rises above him (see page 27).

Graben. U1 and U3 to Stephansplatz.

PIARISTENKIRCHE (Church of the Piarists)

One of the most aesthetically pleasing churches outside the Inner City is that of the Piarists' church in the Josefstadt. The elegant convex façade is thought to follow the plans of Ignaz Dientzenhofer, and the church was probably completed by Matthias Gerl in 1753. The interior is, if anything, even more, impressive,

Pallas Athene Fountain

with its two oval chapels in the transept. The superb cycle of frescos is by Franz Anton Maulbertsch, and represents Biblical themes from Adam and Eve to the Assumption of the Virgin Mary (see page 33).

Jodok-Fink-Platz. Tram J to Strozzigasse.

POSTSPARKASSENAMT (Austrian Post Office Savings Bank)

Georg Coch, whose statue stands in the square in front of the bank, studied English and other models before founding the Austrian Post Office Savings Bank in 1883. In 1903 a competition was held for a new, suitably dignified building for an institution that had come of age. It was won by Otto Wagner, who erected this subsequently famous building, which was finished in 1912. It is one of the most interesting examples of functional elements or materials being deliberately employed for aesthetic effect.

Georg-Coch-Platz 2. Accessible during normal working hours. Trams 1 and 2, U3 to Dr-Karl-Lueger-Platz/Stubentor.

Prater

The legendary Prater is traversed by a magnificent chestnut avenue, 4km long, the scene of social display in the Biedermeier period and later of the workers' May Day marches. With the latter, the Prater could be said to have run the social gamut: it began life as Maximilian II's closely guarded game reserve in 1560 and was opened to the public by Joseph II in 1766; by the time of the World Exhibition, held here in 1873, it was already on the way to becoming the playground of the Viennese.

The Prater still accommodates a wide range of society, from the Golf Club and Jockey Club, to the trotting races, and the cyclodrome and football stadium.

For most people, however, it is the Volks or Wurstelprater that provides the classic image of the Prater – a gigantic fun-fair with everything from dodgems to a ghost train. No visit to Vienna is complete without a ride on the Riesenrad (Big Wheel), designed by an Englishman, that was made unforgettable by the encounter here between Harry Lime and his old friend in the film *The Third Man*. The wheel is 67m high and offers a wonderful view of Vienna from the top of its arc. The entire rotation takes about 20 minutes. Open: from the end of February to the end of November and over Christmas, daily 10am–10pm. In Summer 9am–11pm (particularly crowded on Sundays).

If you've seen The Third Man, *you must try the big wheel*

Make sure you only have a light meal before taking to the roundabout

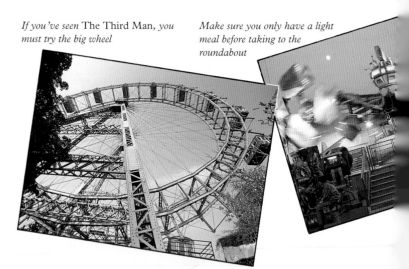

The view from the top is spectacular

All the fun of the fair can be found at the Prater

The Prater illuminated at night

The neo–gothic Rathaus

RATHAUS (City Hall)

When the competition for the new City Hall was announced in 1868, the area between the University and the Parlament was a mass of churned up mud where the cavalry exercised. The winner, Friedrich von Schmidt, wanted to place his grand concept where the Stadtpark is today, but was persuaded by the powerful Liberal mayor of the day, Cajetan Felder, that it would look just as well here. Schmidt's massive building, completed in 1873, represents the apotheosis of neo-gothic architecture, with its open arcades, loggias, balconies, lancet windows and sumptuous statuary. The front elevation is dominated by a 98m tower, on the summit of which stands the Rathausmann, a Renaissance figure bearing a flag, who is the city mascot (in fact based on a representation of the Emperor Maximilian). In the magnificent Banqueting Hall exhibitions and fairs are sometimes held, while in the arcaded courtyard and on the square in front of the building, there are performances during the summer music festival in July and August. For a month before Christmas it is also the location for the popular Christmas Fair. *Rathausplatz, (front entrance). Trams 1 and 2, U2. Tel: 40 00-81 824. Guided tours Monday to Friday at 1pm (except on session days).*

THE RINGSTRASSE – a boulevard encircling the old city

In 1857 the Emperor Francis Joseph made the formal announcement that had long been urged on him by his Minister of the Interior, Alexander Bach: namely, that the elaborate fortifications that had corseted the Inner City since the days of the Turkish menace, together with the military *glacis* (exercise grounds) in front of them, should be done away with. In their place a luxurious boulevard was to be built, flanked by the great representative buildings of the Liberal era. In the next half century Vienna was substantially transformed into the city we know today. Successful entrepreneurs built huge apartment blocks along the Ring, often, like the architect Hansen, occupying the *belle étage* themselves and renting out the other apartments for substantial sums.

But what really stamped the project as the expression of a new political awareness and economic dispensation were the public buildings in symbolic 'Historicist' style – the Parlament by Hansen as Classical Revival, recalling Athenian democracy; the neo-gothic

City Hall by Friedrich von Schmidt, recalling the economically autonomous cities of Flanders in the 15th century; the neo-Renaissance University, and neo-baroque Burgtheater.

Nowadays the fiakers are enveloped in exhaust fumes of tourist buses as they trot round the Ring, and the pedestrian walkway, where Sigmund Freud made his entire round of the Ring daily, is criss-crossed with whizzing cyclists. The best solution for the tourist is to take Trams 1 or 2 and circulate slowly to enjoy the views.

ROMAN RUINS

The Roman camp of *Vindobona* occupied an area north of the Graben (the southern peripheral ditch), and stretched to near Rotenturmstrasse in the east and Tiefer Graben in the west. Outside the camp there was an extensive civil town in the 3rd and 4th centuries, remains of which have been excavated on the Michaelerplatz. (The plan was to leave these open, but unfortunately they are to be covered.)

The Roman supremacy lasted from 15BC (when *Vindobona* was chosen as a subsidiary garrison to nearby Carnuntum on the Danube) until AD433, when Pannonia was ceded to the Huns.

Roman ruins under the Hoher Markt

Just off the Hoher Markt Roman officers' houses were discovered during post-war reconstruction work. In 1950 they were made accessible to the public, their most interesting feature being the hypocaust central heating system (see page 25).
Tel: 53 55 606. U1 and U3 to Stephansplatz. Open: Tuesday to Sunday 9am–12.15 and 1pm–4.30pm.

Roman ruins Am Hof

The remains of a Roman sewer, together with plans and photographs are on display.
Am Hof 9. Tel: 535 55 606. Open: weekends and holidays 11am–1pm. Trams 1 and 2. U2 to Schottentor.

The Ringstrasse circles the city

RUSSISCHES BEFREIUNGS-DENKMAL (Russian Liberation Monument)

As the Russian army battled, plundered and raped its way westwards at the end of the last war, its masters were quick to impress upon the inhabitants of the 'liberated' zones the debt they owed to Soviet military prowess. In Vienna, as elsewhere, a heroic monument was erected with surprising alacrity – this one showing an unknown Red Army soldier, flag in hand, elevated in front of a balustrade, at each end of which are groups of fighting warriors. The Viennese were unimpressed and referred to the soldier as 'The Unknown Plunderer' or the 'The Unknown Rapist'. With the collapse of the Soviet Union there is now discussion as to whether the monument should be demolished (see page 30).
Schwarzenbergplatz. Trams 1 and 2.

The resilient Servitenkirche

SALESIANERINNENKIRCHE (Church of the Salesians)

The Dowager Empress Amalia Wilhelmine, widow of the Emperor Joseph I, called the Salesian nuns to Vienna in 1716. Next to their convent, a school for the daughters of the nobility was set up, in which the Empress also had her lodgings. The unhappy Amalia was from a converted German ducal family and far too pious for the promiscuous Joseph I, who infected her with venereal disease. Political manoeuvrings after his death led to her isolation.

The fine church (1719) is the work of Donato Felice d'Allio, with a façade by Fischer von Erlach the Younger. The baroque interior is particularly rich.
Rennweg 10. Tram 71 from Schwarzenbergplatz.

SERVITENKIRCHE (Servite Church)

The building of the present church began in 1651, sponsored by Prince Piccolomini, an imperial general, and built by Carlo Canevale. It is historically interesting as a baroque survival from before the Turkish siege of 1683 and as the first oval church in Vienna. The stucco work of the two chapels by the entrance is exquisite (see page 37).
Servitengasse 9. Tram D along Porzellangasse to Berggasse stop.

SEZESSION (The Secession Building)

Until 1897, artistic style in 19th-century Vienna had been dominated by the teaching in the Academy of Fine Arts, together with the exhibitions of the Society of Fine Arts in the Künstlerhaus. The latter had degenerated into a closed shop designed to further the financial

The severe face of Sezession

interests of mostly lesser gifted artists of the elder generation. If the works of talented younger artists were exhibited at all, they were carefully relegated to obscure corners or spots just below the ceiling requiring field glasses for close inspection. Retribution came in 1897 when a group of the younger artists dramatically broke away from the society (hence the term Secession) and set up their own grouping, which is generally known by the name 'The Viennese Secession'.

Under the leadership of Gustav Klimt and with the backing of the industrialist Karl Wittgenstein (father of the philosopher Ludwig Wittgenstein), the new society built its own exhibition hall (somewhat cheekily, right next to the Academy of Fine Arts). This unusual 'Grove of Art', as it was envisaged, was the work of Joseph Maria Olbrich and is one of the most famous landmarks of the city. It has severely geometrical proportions, gilded lettering and

decoration on white walls, and is topped by a gilded globe of entwined laurel leaves. On the left of the entrance, in gilt letters, are the words *Ver Sacrum* (Sacred Spring – the title of the Secession's journal); and above the door a motto: 'To the age its art, to art its freedom.' (See page 35.)
Friedrichstrasse 12. Tel: 587 53 07. Open: Tuesday to Friday 10am–6pm, weekends and public holidays 10am–4pm. Trams 1 and 2, U1, U2, U4 to Karlsplatz/Oper.

SIGMUND-FREUD-MUSEUM (Freud's House)

Freud's apartment was on the mezzanine floor at no 5. Number 6, opposite, was his consulting-room, and is now a museum. It contains the famous couch, and antiquities collected by Freud. Much, mostly wasted, academic energy has been expended trying to attach psychological significance to the bric-a-brac (see page 37).
Berggasse 19. Tel: 31 15 96. Open: daily 9am–3pm. Tram D to Berggasse from Schottentor.

Schloss Schönbrunn

(Schönbrunn Palace)

*T*he origins of the great imperial palace of Schönbrunn lie in the 16th century when the Emperor Maximilian II acquired an estate near the village of Hietzing and turned it into a hunting reserve. Under the Emperor Matthias, in the 17th century, an outflow of healing water was discovered here; it was subsequently adorned with water sprites and gave its name to the whole area – Schönbrunn or 'Beautiful Spring'.

In 1692 Johann Bernhard Fischer von Erlach, then architectural tutor to the future Emperor Joseph I, drew up an incredibly ambitious plan for a palace at Schönbrunn to rival Versailles; it was to be situated on the top of the hill, where the Gloriette now stands, and presented a vista of unparalleled splendour with multiple waterfalls, fountains, jousting lists and so forth. However, a more modest plan was ultimately adopted, whereby the palace was removed to the valley of the River Wien and the architectural bombast scaled down. The work proceeded hesitantly, not least because Joseph I died young and Charles VI regarded Schönbrunn as no more than a hunting lodge.

The classical style of the Gloriette

Opening times Ceremonial rooms of the palace, (accessible in guided groups only): April to June, October, daily 8.30am–5pm. July to September, daily 8.30am–5.30pm. November to March, daily 9am–4pm. Tel: 811 13.
Tram 58 from Burgring. U4 from Karlsplatz/Oper to Schönbrunn.

Richly ornate Schönbrunn salon

Maria Theresa and Schönbrunn

It was Maria Theresa who gave the real impetus to the creation of the palace we know today by commissioning her court architect, Nikolaus Pacassi, to convert it into a noble residence. The work lasted from 1744 to 1749; when it was complete, Schönbrunn became the Empress's favourite retreat for herself and her family. It became also more than just a palace, a kind of focus for the peoples of the Empire. Everywhere from Trieste to Czernowitz 'Schönbrunn yellow' was painted on the representative buildings.

'Schönbrunn German', compounded of German, Viennese dialect and French imported words, was the language spoken by the imperial family and imitated elsewhere.

The Palace

Visits are allowed only in groups to limit wear and tear caused by a throughput of some 11,000 visitors daily in the season. The more interesting parts of the tour are as follows:

Francis Joseph's study (Room 4) where the Emperor died in the spartan iron bed in this room on 20 November 1916. This was not quite the end of the Habsburg Empire, but it was certainly the end of an era. A portrait of him on his death-bed by Franz Matsch hangs on the wall along with a portrait of Crown Prince Rudolf.

The Breakfast-room (Room 13) has considerable charm and contains embroidery that is thought to be the work of Maria Theresa's daughters. She had 16 children altogether, of whom three daughters lived only a short while. Two of her sons, Joseph and Leopold, subsequently became emperor. Her second youngest child, Marie Antoinette, married the French Dauphin and was executed in the French Revolution.

The Mirror Room (Room 16) is where Mozart and his sister played before the imperial family, the six-year-old prodigy boldly announcing that he would marry one of the Empress's daughters.

The Ceremonial Hall (Room 24) has a large portrait of Maria Theresa by Van Meytens.

The Vieux-Laque-Zimmer (Room 26) is particularly fine, with a marquetry floor, black lacquer panels and a portrait of Franz Stephan of Lorrain, Maria Theresa's husband. He did much to put the perennially shaky Habsburg finances in order, and the marriage was proverbially happy, although he was a philanderer.

The Millionen-Zimmer (Room 29) is so-called because it was supposed to have cost a million to build. It is decorated with 260 17th-century Persian and Indian miniatures in rococo frames. With its playful gilded richness, the room represents the apotheosis of the rococo interior as it appealed to contemporary aristocratic taste.

SCHLOSS SCHÖNBRUNN

The elaborately decorated theatre

Schönbrunner Schlosstheater

In the northwest corner of the ceremonial courtyard Maria Theresa had Pacassi build a small theatre, chiefly so that her numerous talented children could give family performances of singing, dancing and recitation. The rococo theatre's interior was remodelled in 1767 by Ferdinand von Hohenberg. Later it saw performances of French classics during the brief period when Napoleon made Schönbrunn his headquarters in the occupations of 1805 and 1809. Today it is the venue for acting seminars for aspirant performers, and a summer season by the Wiener Kammeroper.

The Wagenburg (Carriage Museum)

Southwest of the courtyard is the Carriage Museum, with an interesting collection of items; it includes an imperial coach built in the 18th century, various carriages used by the imperial family and leading aristocrats for state or other occasions and the hearse used at Francis Joseph's funeral. It also contains sleighs, coaching liveries, harnesses and other accoutrements.

The chapel in the east wing is open on Sundays (usually) and dates to 1695, with alterations in 1744. The ceiling fresco is by Daniel Gran, but the most important works are the altar picture by Paul Troger, of *The Wedding of Mary* and a tabernacle relief by Georg Raphael Donner. The Bergl-Zimmer rooms to the left of the main entrance may be seen only on request. The room is decorated with landscape murals by a Bohemian artist, Johann Wenzel Bergl, which were painted between 1769 and 1777.

The magnificent Neptune's Fountain

The Park

Schönbrunn's Park was laid out by a Frenchman, Jean Trehet, and later altered by a landscape gardener from Holland named Adrian van Steckhoven. Although it retains baroque features, such as the rigid and unnatural cutting back of the trees along the allées, it is now more of a Romantic landscape garden, complete with sentimental allusions to antiquity. Ferdinand von Hohenberg supplied most of these – the fake Roman ruins for instance, the cascade and obelisk, and above all the Gloriette. This piece of architectural bombast – a stone pavilion surmounted

A view of Vienna from the Gloriette

by an eagle with outstretched wings – crowns the steep mound that rises behind the palace. It commemorates the battle of Kolin (1757) when Maria Theresa had at last introduced sufficient competence in the higher echelons of the armed forces to beat Frederick II of Prussia on the battlefield.

The Palmhouse and Tiergarten

To the west of the palace is the splendid Palmhouse, erected in 1882 and rivalling those at Kew as the most spectacular 19th-century iron and glass constructions still standing. Beyond it is the Tiergarten (zoo) which has a long history reaching back to the Emperor Maximilian's fondness for collecting animals. It is, however, beginning to show its age and there is increasing pressure from animal lovers to have it reformed, or better still, dissolved. The current plan is to privatise it.

Opening times:

Park: daily 6am until dusk. Carriage Museum: May to September, Tuesday to Sunday 10am–5pm. October to April, Tuesday to Sunday 10am–4pm. Tel: 82 32 44. Zoo: daily, 9am until dusk (but not later than 6pm). Tel: 877 12 36 or 877 92 94. Gloriette: May to October, daily 8am–6pm. Palmhouse: in summer, daily 9am–6pm; in winter, 9am–3pm. Tel: 877 50 87.

SCHÖNBRUNN

Frances Trollope (mother of the novelist Anthony Trollope) describes the River Wien at Schönbrunn in the 1830's:

'It is impossible to believe that one, whose days may be counted by the noble and beautiful works with which she [Maria Theresa] adorned her empire, could have passed to her imperial creation at Schönbrunn within reach of this...black and vilely smelling ditch...and suffered its unhallowed waters to flow between the wind and her regality...'

Statues and Monuments

(For monuments to composers and musicians see pages 84–87)

*A*part from religious statuary, there were few monuments in Vienna up to 1850, and those that there were exclusively represented members of the ruling house or occasionally their generals. Francis Joseph loved statues, however; indeed, they seemed to be the one form of art he really appreciated. So many new monuments were put up between 1850 and 1918 that the coffee-house wits talked of a new plague threatening the city – the Denkmalpest (monument plague). In this period artists, poets and scientists were honoured; and later, even politicians.

The following is a selection only, of statues, monuments and fountains that may be of aesthetic or historical interest to the visitor. A few which are of major significance occur elsewhere.

ABSTRACT

The Henry Moore Fountain ('Hill Arches') – in front of the St Charles Church. This statue was a gift of the English sculptor to Vienna in 1978.

CULTURAL FIGURES

Goethe-Monument – Opernring
This is the work of Edmund Hellmer (1900). A massive representation of the genius loftily regarding the world from his chair.

Goethe–Monument, Opernring

Grillparzer Monument – Volksgarten
Homage is paid here to Austria's national poet and dramatist, Franz Grillparzer (1791–1872). On the back of the enclosing wall are scenes from his plays in relief.

Lessing Monument – Judenplatz
Gotthold Ephraim Lessing, the author of *Nathan the Wise Man*, is appropriately honoured here on the site of the old ghetto. This and other monuments with Jewish associations were destroyed by the Nazis, but erected again after the war.

Makart Monument – Stadtpark
Hans Makart (1840–1884) was the most celebrated painter of 'Historicism' in the 'Foundation Period' of the late 19th century. The artist is shown wearing the costume he designed for the great pageant he organised to celebrate Francis Joseph's and Elisabeth's Silver Wedding in 1879.

Ressel Monument – Resselpark
Josef Ressel (1783–1857) invented the

ship's screw in 1827; however, like other creative minds of his day, he fell victim to the obtuse censorship of Metternich's régime, and was forbidden to develop his idea.

Schiller Monument – Schillerplatz

This is a monument to Friedrich von Schiller, one of the greatest German poets and dramatists. The work is by Johann Schilling of Dresden, unveiled in 1876.

EQUESTRIAN STATUES

Two of the most striking are of successful generals: Archduke Carl and Prince Eugene of Savoy on the Heldenplatz, both by Anton Fernkorn (see page 71).

Archduke Albrecht Monument – Augustinerbastei

The Habsburg general is honoured for leading Austrian troops to victory at Custozza, Italy, in 1866.

Emperor Joseph II Monument – Josefsplatz

A bronze equestrian representation of the enlightened emperor (1780–1790) as Marcus Aurelius, after the statue on the Capitol in Rome.

Schwarzenberg Monument – Schwarzenbergplatz

The subject is Field Marshall Karl Philipp, Prince Schwarzenberg, 'victorious leader of the allied forces against Napoleon in 1813 and 1814'.

THE IMPERIAL HOUSE
The Empress Elisabeth Monument – Volksgarten

Erected on the initiative of the populace in 1902, after her assassination in 1898.

The Emperor Francis Joseph Monument – Burggarten

The ageing emperor is shown in the military uniform he perpetually wore.

The Emperor Francis II (I of Austria) Monument – 'In der Burg'

Here again the emperor is presented as a Roman emperor and the work is encrusted with flattering allegorical allusions and inscriptions.

POLITICAL
Lueger Monument – Dr-Karl-Lueger-Platz

The extremely popular anti-Semitic Mayor of Vienna (1897–1910) is celebrated here; allegorical allusions to his achievements in modernising Vienna surround him.

Renner Monument – Rathauspark

The Socialist Karl Renner was chancellor of the First Republic in 1918 and first president of the Second Republic in 1945. The imposing bust is by the well-known sculptor Alfred Hrdlicka.

Monument for the Victims of Fascism – Morzinplatz

The City of Vienna erected this on the site of the Hotel Metropole, which was the headquarters of the Gestapo during the war.

POPULAR LEGEND
Hannakenbrunnen – Am Gestade

The statue is of two men carrying a wounded third. According to the legend, a doctor in the neighbourhood had passers-by attacked, and then brought to him to have their wounds dressed, thus ingeniously increasing his income.

Stephansdom

(The Cathedral and Metropolitan Church of St Stephen the Martyr)

The History of St Stephen's

The finest Gothic building in Austria began life as a relatively modest parish church built just outside the then city walls in the mid-12th century. This originally Romanesque church was consecrated by the Bishop of Passau in 1147; however, most of it was destroyed by fire and the earliest parts of the present building – the Riesentor (Giant's Gate) and Heidentürme (Heathen Towers) – were built around a century later. Under the Habsburgs, the existing Romanesque church was incorporated into a much larger Gothic structure, and the lovely high-Gothic 'Albertine Choir' was built, between 1304 and 1340.

Under Albrecht's son, Rudolf IV 'The Founder', work proceeded apace on the church and the Duke himself laid

Stephansdom, Gothic masterpiece

the foundation stone for the great South Tower in 1358. In the next century, during the reign of Emperor Friedrich III, the vaulting of the nave was completed by the master-craftsman, Hans Puchsbaum, in 1446. The spectacular roof timbers followed and survived until the fire at the end of the last war, when they were replaced with 600 tons of steel supports. The North Tower was begun in 1450, but never completed, and only in 1556 crowned with a Renaissance copper cupola. At the end of World War II St Stephen's caught fire in circumstances that have never been fully clarified. Contributions from all over Austria financed subsequent restoration work.

The Exterior

The Giant's Door and Heathen Towers at the west end of the cathedral survive from the Romanesque period. (The Heathen Towers seem to have been so-called as they looked primitive, or even minaret-like to the inhabitants, while the Giant's Door got its name because the bones of a mammoth – taken to be those of an Ur-Wiener giant – were for some time displayed here). Around the banked arches of the door are vivid sculptures featuring biblical motifs and grotesques.

The South Tower is known to the Viennese as the 'Steffl' and was completed in 1433 after constant building for some 75 years. The third highest spire in Europe after Ulm and Cologne, it is the city's most beloved landmark, and features continuously in depictions of Vienna from the Schottenmeister's panels of 1470 to the lovingly made water-colours of Rudolph von Alt at the turn of the century.

It has suffered many vicissitudes – two Turkish cannon balls are still embedded in it and in the 19th century much of it had to be dismantled and rebuilt due to damage from lightning and an earthquake. For those who want to climb the tower, which is 136.7m high and has 343 steps, the entry is next to the sacristan's office outside. In the course of the climb you encounter Starhemberg's bench, the look-out post of the garrison commander during the Turkish siege of 1683.

Circling the church anti-clockwise you pass the Singertor, with a depiction of Rudolf IV and a vivid relief of the conversion of St Paul in the tympanum; on the north side is the pulpit (originally Gothic) from which Giovanni Capistrano roused the populace against the Turks. The sandstone fabric of the church now faces a new form of attack after all the fires and wars, namely sulphur dioxide in the air. A continuous programme of renovation is under way to combat this.

THE PUMMERIN

The 'Pummerin' or 'boomer' of St Stephen's now hangs in the Adler (North) Tower and was originally named after the Emperor Joseph I. It was cast from the Turkish cannon abandoned by the besiegers during their headlong flight in 1683; it weighed 17,000kg and the clapper 813kg. As the Russian forces entered the city in 1945, St Stephen's caught fire and the huge bell crashed from its moorings in the South Tower and smashed. A new mega-bell, weighing 20,000kg, was cast from the remains of the old one and other bells damaged in the flames.

STEPHANSDOM

The Interior

Inside St Stephen's there is a rich array of artistic masterpieces of the Gothic, Renaissance and baroque ages (some 34 Gothic altars vanished in the barockisation phase). The first impression of length and mass is arresting, the main nave being 107m long and 39m high, with reticulated vaulting. Most of the lovely Gothic stained-glass panels were lost in the 1945 fire, but four remain in the side window of the choir near the altar – on the southern side is a graphic stoning of St Stephen. The most important works are as follows:

Anton Pilgram's Pulpit, 1510, on the left of the nave, not far from the entrance. This is one of the most vivid and powerful masterpieces of late Gothic to survive. On the parapet are the four fathers of the church.

Pilgram surveys his work

Anton Pilgram's pulpit

On the balustrade crawl lizards and toads, symbols of good and evil, and perhaps also a reminder to the preacher not to be puffed up by applause for his performance. From below the pulpit steps Anton Pilgram leans out of a window surveying his handiwork, an almost unique contemporary example of an artist positioning himself at the heart of his work.

On a column near by is the popular *Servant's Madonna*, so-called because a falsely accused servant-girl successfully appealed to it to clear her name.

The Foot of the Organ Loft (on the wall of the north aisle) has an even more lively depiction of Pilgram, where all the stone ribs coalesce and appear to be resting on the master's back. Again he leans out of a window, with a quizzical look, bowed down by the weight of his own creation, yet triumphantly the master of it.

In the north apse (the 'Ladies' Choir') is a remarkable Gothic wing altar from Wiener Neustadt with carved scenes of the Virgin Mary and the life of Christ, and 72 saints painted on the exterior.

The High Altar was commissioned in 1641 from Johann Pöck. The focal point of his elaborately iconographical architecture is his brother Tobias's version of the stoning of St Stephen.

The Tomb of Emperor Friedrich III is in the south apse, the most spectacular surviving Renaissance work in Vienna. It is executed in red marble to a design by

Niklas Gerhaert van Leyden, who died in 1493, while working on it. It was completed in 1513.

Unfortunately, the finest part of the work – Gerhaert's carving of Frederick in coronation robes on the lid of the tomb – cannot be seen as it is too high, but the side friezes and balustrade can be. The tomb is accessible with guided tours only.

To the northeast of the cathedral is the Archbishop's Palais, and next to it the Dom- und Diözesanmuseum (Cathedral and Diocesan Museum – entrance Stephansplatz 6 in the courtyard). It contains numerous treasures and paintings by Cranach, Rottmayr, Maulbertsch and others. The portrait of Rudolf IV is the first recorded in the German-speaking world.

Open: Wednesday to Saturday 10am–6pm, Sunday 10am–4pm. Tel: 515 52-578. U1 and U3 to Stephansplatz.

Visits to the main body of the church in a guided group: Monday to Saturday 10.30am and 3pm; Sundays and holidays 3pm. June to September, evening tours also, Saturday at 7pm. July and August also Friday, 7pm.

For Catacombs see page 115 (visits daily 10am–11.30am and 2pm–4.30pm). Pummerin in the North Tower, daily 9am–5.30pm. Ascent of South Tower, March to October, daily 9am–5.30pm; November to February, 9am–4.30pm. Tel: 515 52-563 (see page 28).

The Nave and High Altar

Subterranean Vienna

A visitor to Vienna in the 15th century, Aeneas Silvius Piccolomini remarked that 'almost as much of the town was below ground as was above it.' Naturally the expansion of the city has turned this observation into no more than a flight of fancy, but it is still true that Vienna has plenty of spectacular sights under the surface – crypts, baroque wine cellars, even the sewers that featured so dramatically in the film of *The Third Man*.

An ornate sarcophagus at Kaisergruft

Habsburg Necrolatry

In the 17th century the Austrian branch of the Habsburgs acquired some of the bizarre customs of their Spanish counterparts, particularly in matters like court etiquette and funeral ritual.

Thus, the practice arose of carving up the bodies of the Emperors on death and distributing the bits and pieces around the city: the hearts were kept in silver urns in the Augustines' Church, the entrails in bronze boxes in the catacombs of St Stephen and the rest of them in the sarcophagi in the Imperial Crypt of the Capuchin Church.

The Capuchin Crypt

The Kaisergruft (Imperial Burial Vault) was instituted by the wife of the Emperor Matthias. Since 1633, when he and his wife were laid to rest here, some 12 emperors and 17 empresses have followed him, the last being the Empress Zita buried in 1989 with a semi-state funeral. The most ornate baroque sarcophagi are by Balthasar Moll (for Maria Theresa's parents and for Maria Theresa herself and her husband, Franz Stephan).

Following death, the imperial corpses were opened, the entrails and heart extracted, then filled with wax before being sewn up and deposited here.

When the hearse arrived at the door, a question and answer ritual with the Prior ensued. Only when the Lord Chamberlain dropped all the emperor's titles, and craved admittance for a 'humble sinner' was the body allowed in (see page 58).

Neuer Markt. Kaisergruft – open: daily 9.30am–4pm. Tel: 512 68 53-12.

The Catacombs of St Stephen – Stephansdom

In 1732 burials ceased in the graveyard which then existed around St Stephen's and a new crypt was built from 1745. Bodies from the great plagues of 1348, 1679 and 1713 had been hastily buried here.

When the chambers were full, convicts and penitents were employed to wash and stack the bones of the decayed remains, in order to make more room. The Ducal Crypt under the Albertine Choir has 18 niches closed with wrought-iron gates, with 56 chests for entrails (see page 28).

The entrance is near the organ loft by Pilgram on the north side. Catacombs of St Stephen's: open daily 10am–11.30am and 2pm–4.30pm.

The Crypt of St Michael's Church

Steep steps descend to the burial vaults of the church, occupied by members of the aristocracy and court servants. Some half dozen of the coffin lids have lifted, displaying the mummified remains of the occupants with leathery skin and moth-eaten clothes – the climatic conditions of the vault having partly preserved them. (see page 23).

Michaelerplatz. Michaelergruft – open: Monday to Saturday 11am and 3pm; Sunday 11am.

Wine Cellars

Of the many wine-cellars in Vienna it is worth visiting the deep Twelve Apostles' Cellar at Sonnenfelsgasse no 3, which sinks two storeys through a baroque level to a medieval one. The Urbanikeller am Hof, the Esterhazykeller at Haarhof no 1 and the Melker Stiftskeller at Schotten-gasse no 3, likewise offer a medieval or baroque below-ground experience to be enjoyed with the local wine.

In addition there is a selection of underground tours advertised in the monthly programme obtainable from the Tourist Information Bureau. They include: Medieval Vienna above and below ground; Unknown Vienna below ground; Death in Vienna; Burial places and the Death Cult; and a Tour of the Sewers organised by the City Hall.

The Esterhazykeller, Haarhof no 1

The art nouveau Strudlhofstiege

STRUDLHOFSTIEGE

The complicated name of this remarkable piece of street architecture goes back to the court painter Peter von Strudel (1648-1714), who built himself a 'Hof' near here in 1690. The 'Strudlhof' served as atelier and also housed his extensive collection of pictures. Works by him and his brother are to be found in many of the churches and noble collections of Vienna.

Strudlhofgasse is a cul-de-sac ending at the edge of a precipitous drop to Liechtensteinstrasse. In 1910 the marvellous art nouveau steps joining the two streets were built to a design by Theodor Jäger. They have acquired a special, almost shrine-like significance in the Viennese consciousness since Heimito von Doderer published his great novel of Vienna life in 1951, itself entitled *Die Strudlhofstiege*. The novel explores the enduring traditions of the bureaucratic class and uses the famous steps as a topographical and spiritual backdrop to the action of the story (see page 37).

Between Strudlhofgasse and Liechtensteinstrasse. Trams 38, 40, 41, 42 along Währinger Strasse to the junction with Nussdorfer Strasse

SYNAGOGUE

In 1826 Josef Kornhäusel, one of the leading architects of neo-classicism, built the 'City Temple' for the Jewish community. According to the prescripts still in force since Joseph II's Edict of Toleration, the façades of non-Catholic religious buildings were not to betray their functions (the Protestants were forbidden to build towers or spires for their churches). The synagogue thus appears from the outside to be a dwelling house.

The interior is an imposing oval space with a cupola, and has a gallery running round it, above white Ionic columns. The left-hand entrance to the house leads to the recently opened (1900) Jewish Museum.

Tours of the synagogue and museum

are possible by telephone appointment: 531 04-15.
Jewish Community Centre, Seitenstettengasse 4. Trams 1 and 2, U1 and U4 to Schwedenplatz.

TECHNISCHES MUSEUM (Museum of Technology)

It is worth taking the time to visit this outlying museum, which can be combined with nearby Schönbrunn. The graceless and heavy neo-baroque building (by Hans Schneider) replaced the modern competition-winning design by Otto Wagner, which was blocked by the reactionary Archduke Franz Ferdinand, who hated Wagner and all his works. Although completed in 1913, the museum was not opened to the public until 1918.

In the surrounding garden a number of venerable steam locomotives have been placed. The interior offers a fascinating chronological survey of industrial development in Austria, and the achievements of Austrian scientists, engineers and inventors. It serves to remind the visitor that the disproportionate contributions to culture by 'Austrian' humanist intellectuals in the modern era, had its counterpart in the hard sciences, although structural and political difficulties often meant that the latter successes were undervalued.

Among the most interesting displays are a history of mining, details of the bent-wood furniture manufacture of the Thonet firm, early cars and locomotives, musical instruments and a history of the post. There is even a baroque 'writing machine' designed by Friedrich von Knaus in 1760, and a typewriter of 1864. It is now planned to renovate the entire museum so that it is unfortunately likely to be closed for some time.

Mariahilfer Strasse 212. Tel: 891 01. Open: Tuesday to Sunday 9am–4.30pm. Trams 52 and 58.

THESEUSTEMPEL (Theseion)

Peter von Nobile built this scaled down replica of the so-called 'Theseion' in Athens in 1823. (In fact the Athens building has subsequently been identified as the Temple of Hephaistos and Athena.) Originally it contained Antonio Canova's heroic *Theseus* sculpture, now on the stairway of the Museum of Fine Arts. The temple was at first intended to house antique works of art, but is now used for exhibitions of modern painting and sculpture (see page 22).
Volksgarten. Trams 1 and 2 to Dr-Karl-Renner-Ring.

The Theseustempel houses modern paintings and sculptures in the Volksgarten

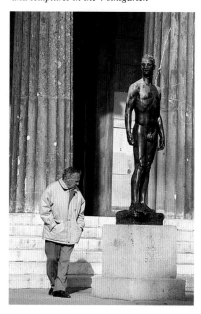

Vienna's Gothic Votivkirche

shows the excavation, which is 12m below street level, and was probably the crypt for an even older burial chapel. There is a small exhibition of ceramics in it.

Stephansplatz. Tel: 52 20-503. Open: daily except Monday 9am–12.15 and 1pm–4.30pm. U1 and U3 to Stephansplatz.

VOTIVKIRCHE

This, the greatest Gothic church of Vienna, was built as a thanksgiving for the narrow escape of Francis Joseph from an assassination attempt. As he was walking on the bastions on 18 February, 1853, a Hungarian tailor attacked him with a knife; the Emperor was saved by the metal button on the collar of his tunic. At the suggestion of his brother, the ill-fated later Emperor of Mexico, a competition was announced for the building of a votive church, which had to be Gothic. The 27-year-old Heinrich Ferstel won against 74 other entries.

After a site on the Belvedere heights was abandoned, the Votivkirche became the first building of the Ringstrasse era to be initiated, in 1856, although it was not completed until 1879. The long duration of the building works was largely due to Ferstel's insistence on the use of traditional craftsman techniques and his perfectionism with regard to materials. Ferstel took as his model the finest medieval cathedrals of France and Germany, and provided a new Viennese landmark with his twin steeples, worked to soaring points of exquisite filigree carving. The interior is overpainted in warm muted colours. The church possesses the Renaissance tomb (1533) of Count Salm by Loy Hering. The Count was the commander of the garrison in the 1529 Turkish siege (see

VIRGILKAPELLE

In the cemetery that surrounded the west and southwest of St Stephen's from the Middle Ages up to the 18th century there seem to have been two chapels over the years, one built over the other. The later of these, the Maria Magdalena Chapel, was demolished following a fire in 1781. When the U-Bahn was being built in 1972, 13th-century remains of both were discovered, together with a charnel house. A picture-window on your left, as you descend to the metro,

page 36).
Rooseveltplatz. Trams 1 and 2, U2 to Schottentor.

WITTGENSTEIN-HAUS

The Wittgenstein House – which is now the Bulgarian Cultural Institute and accessible during exhibitions – was built in 1928 by Paul Engelmann, a pupil of Adolf Loos. The philosopher Ludwig Wittgenstein also assisted with the design (the house was for his sister). It is considered a fine example of 'functionalism'.
Kundmanngasse 19, Parkgasse 18. U3 to Rochusgasse.

WOTRUBAKIRCHE

The Holy Trinity Church designed by Fritz Wotruba is probably the most remarkable piece of post-war architecture (1976) in Vienna. From the outside it appears as an ordered, yet unpredictable mass of geometrical beton slabs; in the spaces between them are similarly severe geometrical panels of plate-glass. The architect wrote: 'The aim is: order – law – harmony, a community consists of single individuals. If the community is a happy one, then it can be regarded as harmonious. That is the problem of our age and of the church. This building should demonstrate that chaos can only be overcome through law and order. This is the pre-condition for survival.'
Maurer Lange Gasse 137. This is a long way out: take Tram 60 from Hietzing to the junction with Endresstrasse in Mauer, then Bus 60A to end stop.

Wotrubakirche's geometrical design

Getting away from it all

PARKS, GARDENS AND CEMETERIES

In the 17th and 18th centuries many of the aristocracy liked to build themselves two palaces in Vienna, one for the winter months, and a summer, or 'garden-palais' outside the Inner City. Some of these gardens still exist, although many are sadly decayed; but the Liechtenstein Palais (see page 37) still gives an idea of the baroque summer life-style. The Belvedere gardens (page 49) and Schönbrunn Park (page 106) are the best kept of the once private demesnes, although they too have undergone considerable change since they were first laid out.

Relaxing in the Burggarten

AUGARTEN

Aulandschaft is the term used for the meadowland and swamp along the banks of the Danube; in the past it was frequently flooded. The area was turned into a hunting reserve under Emperor Matthias and Charles VI commissioned Jean Trehet (responsible also for Schönbrunn) to lay out the park in 1712. At the end of the 17th century the present palace was built, although it was subsequently much altered; it now houses the Vienna Boys Choir. The so-called Saalgebäude is the base for the famous Augarten porcelain manufactory, originally founded in the 18th century under imperial patronage. Porcelain Lipizzaner horses have proved to be their most successful export.

Joseph II, repeating a gesture he made elsewhere, threw open the gardens to the public in 1775. He also had Isidor Canevale build an architectural folly named after himself (the Joseph-Stöckl – a sort of antique tower). Canevale built the triumphal arch over the entrance, above which are inscribed the words: 'A pleasure park dedicated to all men by one who esteems them.' Mozart, Beethoven and Johann Strauss Sr all gave concerts here, and it was the venue for glittering events during the Congress of Vienna .

Second District. Guided tours of the Augarten porcelain factory: April to September, Monday, Tuesday and Wednesday 9.30am. Admission charge. Tram N from Schwedenplatz along Taborstrasse.

BURGGARTEN

After the Napoleonic troops had blown up the bastions round the Hofburg in 1809, the authorities made a virtue of necessity and laid out two new gardens, the Volksgarten (see page 122) and the Burggarten, then known as the Kaisergarten. The architect, Louis von Remy, planned it as an intimate sanctuary with winding paths and luxurious flower beds. In 1826 one of the earliest glasshouses was built here, the present impressive one, on the same site, being a later construction by Friedrich Ohmann in 1907, in steel and glass with Jugendstil ornamentation.

The Burggarten contains the Mozart Monument and other notable memorials (see pages 108–9) and would be the pleasantest place to sit out in summer were it not for the fact that some parts of it have been colonised by the drug fraternity.

Between the Neue Hofburg, Hanuschgasse,

Goethegasse and Opernring. Trams 1 and 2 to Burgring.

STADTPARK

The Stadtpark's neo-baroque Kursalon

Part of the area now occupied by the City Park was already a favoured recreation area in the Biedermeier period. In the summer evenings Johann Strauss Sr and his orchestra sometimes played here and there was a temple-like building where curative waters were dispensed. At the beginning of the Ringstrasse era, the Liberal mayor of the day, Dr Andreas Zelinka, energetically promoted the idea of a city park – in this case built by and for the burghers.

The park was laid out in the English landscape style by Rudolf Siebeck and a painter, Josef Selleny, who designed its winding paths, ornamental ponds and miniature waterfalls. It contains many busts and statues of famous artists and musicians, including Schubert, Makart, Schindler, Bruckner and Johann Strauss, The neo-baroque 'Kursalon' houses the main casino in Vienna.

Parkring 3, Heumarkt. Trams 1 and 2 to Parkring.

TÜRKENSCHANZPARK

West of the so-called cottage area and north of the Sternwarte (astronomical observatory) is to be found this lesser-known park, which was created on the initiative of the architect Heinrich Ferstel. It was laid out in the English style on a hilly site, and originally had two bandstands, a restaurant and an observation tower. No lesser person than Francis Joseph himself opened it in 1885 and delivered a keynote speech that was to lead to the integration of outlying suburbs into the borough of Vienna.

Peace and quiet in the Volksgarten

The curious name of the park means 'Turkish trench': one line of the attackers' trenches was built here during the siege of 1683. A crescent moon over the entrance recalls this association, and in 1922 two mass graves dating from the siege were discovered here.
Gregor-Mendel-Strasse, Hasenauerstrasse, Max-Emanuel-Strasse. Tram 41 from Schottentor to Türkenschanzplatz.

VOLKSGARTEN

Like the Burggarten, the Volksgarten (or People's Garden) owes its origin to the destruction of the bastions in 1809 by the French, but was begun much later in 1821. The area was actually an extension of Maria Theresa's *Paradeisgartel*, so-called because Paradeiser (Austrian German for tomatoes) were grown there; it was thus actually the kitchen garden for the court, not, as is sometimes thought, a 'Paradise Garden'.

It was decided to lay out the gardens in the rigid and already outmoded French style, instead of in the intimate English style of the (still private) Burggarten. This decision followed objections from the authorities that public order required an open layout to remove immorality or criminality, which might occur under cover of English-style bushes. The gardens contain the Theseion, a coffee-house and a dance-hall, together with some interesting monuments and statues (see pages 22, 108–9 and 117).
Dr-Karl-Renner-Ring, Löwelstrasse, Heldenplatz. Trams 1 and 2 to Dr.-Karl-Renner-Ring.

CEMETERIES OF VIENNA

HIETZINGER FRIEDHOF

The picturesque cemetery is the last resting place of many distinguished figures of 19th-century Vienna, including the playwright Franz Grillparzer, the artist Gustav Klimt and Francis Joseph's long-standing platonic companion, the actress Katharina Schratt.
Maxingstrasse 15. Bus 56B from Kennedybrücke (U4 to Hietzing).

SANKT MARXER FRIEDHOF

Emperor Joseph II decreed the creation of five communal cemeteries outside the city walls as those inside were full. St Mark's is the only one to survive, and is

attractively rural. Its most famous occupant was Mozart.
Leberstrasse 6–8. Tram 71 from Schwarzenbergplatz to Simmering (Aspangbahn).

ZENTRALFRIEDHOF

The Central Cemetery was opened on All Saints Day 1874, the day of the year when thousands of Viennese still flock there to lay their wreaths on the graves of loved ones or of celebrated figures in the 'Graves of Honour'. Many of the greatest personalities in the sciences and the arts have been transferred or buried here. (A plan may be obtained at the main gate.) It is also worth visiting Max Hegele's monumental church, named after Mayor Karl Lueger, and the nearby crematorium (opposite Gate 2 of the cemetery) to a striking design by Holzmeister.
Simmeringer Hauptstrasse 234.

Burial in style at Central Cemetery

Picturesque graves in Zentralfriedhof

DEATH IN VIENNA

The Viennese passion for a *schöne Leich* (a fine funeral) is legendary: Joseph II aroused more animosity with his institution of *Klappsärgen* (reusable coffins with false bottoms) than with any other measure. Cabaret humour dwells gleefully on the permutations and suggestive potential of expressions for death, and *Heurigen* balladeers wallow, with maudlin relish, on the bitter-sweet prospect of imminent demise. This mixture of morbid counter-reformatory religiosity and a vulgar taste for the macabre meant that death was big business in Vienna, until the abuses of the private undertakers were curbed by Mayor Karl Lueger's founding of a publicly financed firm with fixed prices. Even today, 50 per cent of Viennese opt for the expensive 'First Class Burial' offered by the council.

The Heurigen Tradition

Wine-making in and around Vienna goes back to the times of the Illyrians and Celts, although it was systematised by the Romans. In the late Middle Ages, there existed what is nowadays known as a 'wine lake'; soured wine from the overproduction was applied by imperial decree, for mixing the mortar used in the construction of St Stephen's.

The *Heurige* (wine-tavern) tradition really begins with the ordinances of Joseph II. Vineyard owners were allowed to sell 'this year's' (*heuer*) wine from the family premises until the supply ran out. During that period a bunch of fir twigs is hung outside the door and beside it a plaque with the word *Ausg'steckt*.

In the 19th century the brothers Schrammel added a new ingredient to the '*Heurige*' scene – namely music from a fiddle, a clarinet (now an accordion) and a guitar, which is still a feature of many establishments. The real test of genuineness, however, is the wine: it must be from the *Heurige's* own vineyard, not imported; often it will be the *gemischter Satz*, the produce of mixed grape varieties all grown together. This (mostly white) wine is served in quarter-litre mugs and is light, fruity and petillant. It is not as unalcoholic as it looks.

Indulge in some wine served in a typical tavern

*When you see this sign,
why not step inside?*

*Vineyards outside Vienna
feed the Heurigen tradition*

A delivery of grapes

*Everyone enjoys the
atmosphere that comes
with good wine and food*

A typical Heurigen tavern, Grinzing

VIENNESE WINE PRODUCTION

After a severe decline at the end of the 19th century due to the phylloxera, taxation and the rival attractions of beer and coffee, production has recovered in the 20th century. Today, 700 hectares are planted with vines on the surrounding hills. There are 644 vineyard owners, of whom 185 sell their produce in *Heurigen*. About $2\frac{1}{2}$ million litres of wine are put on the market, almost all of it sold in *Heurigen*.

HEURIGEN VILLAGES

It is a sad, but no doubt inevitable, consequence of tourism that the *Heurige* concept has been abused and exploited in recent years; many an establishment that is got up to look exactly like a *Buschenschenker* (supplier of his own

wine) actually serves hot food like any restaurant, and imports the wine. The crowning insult is unbearable kitsch music from a Hammond organ or the like. Would-be aficionados should bear in mind, also, that there is no such thing as an expensive *Heurige*. Help is at hand, however: the newspapers list genuine *Buschenschenken* under the rubric *Ausg'steckt*; and the wine villages have a sign-tree in the main street, likewise listing all the places currently *Ausg'steckt*.

GRINZING

This is one of the most beloved, and consequently one of the most crowded tourist venues, yet somehow still preserves a lot of the Biedermeier charm of the country village it once was. After a regular horse-carriage service was established between it and the city in 1827, it became a popular excursion

place for the Viennese. Many was the song or poem inspired by soft evenings here on the edge of the Wienerwald: *Ich muss wieder einmal in Grinzing sein, Beim Wein, beim Wein, beim Wein* (For Grinzing, Grinzing do I pine, And wine, oh wine, yes wine...).
Tram 38 from Schottentor. Last tram from Grinzing: 11.48pm.

HEILIGENSTADT

Heiligenstadt is one of the most charming peripheral villages of the city, a fact appreciated by Beethoven who lived in various quarters here. The ancestors of the Mayer family who run the *Heurige* in the 'Beethovenhaus' on Pfarrplatz, settled here at the end of the Turkish siege in 1683 (see page 39).
U4 to Heiligenstadt, then Bus 38B. Last tram back: 12.15pm.

MAUER

On the southwest edge of Vienna are a number of lesser-known wine villages (to the tourist at least) including Rodaun, Kalksburg, Atzgersdorf and Mauer.

Mauer is traditionally the haunt of those who like to drink their wine in peace and enjoy the simplest of traditional locales. There are 12 *Busch–enschenken* in Mauer, three in Rodaun and one each in the other two villages.

Tram 60 from Hietzing to Maurer Lange Gasse. Last tram back 12.16pm.

NEUSTIFT AM WALDE AND SALMANNSDORF

It is hard to imagine that the inhabitants of these two picturesque and peaceful villages were still subject to attacks by wolves from the Wienerwald up to the 18th century. There are numerous *Heurigen* in Neustift and three in Salmannsdorf (see page 41).
Bus 35A from U6 Nussdorfer Strasse to both villages. Tram 38 from Schottentor connects. Last bus back: 11.55pm.

STAMMERSDORF

The village has preserved its rural character to a remarkable degree, close to an otherwise rather industrialised area north of the Danube. The three villages next to the Bisamberg – Jedlersdorf and Strebersdorf are the other two – have preserved the *Heurige* wine tradition that is often elsewhere sullied by 'marketing' for tourism. Consequently there are a great many very small establishments, the prices are low and the guests know their wine.
Tram 31 from Schottenring. Last tram back: 11.28pm.

A popular drinking venue

The Danube provides recreation for the locals while UNO–City watches

ALTE DONAU, DONAUINSEL

As a result of the regulation of the river in the 1870s, the Danube ceased to swamp whole areas around Nussdorf as it had in 1830 and 1862. The Danube Canal, regulated by locks at Nussdorf (1898), skirted the edge of the Inner City. Beyond it was the main flow of the river, now separated from the Alte Donau (Old Danube) which is supplied from the water table. Here there are a number of beaches, traditionally patronised by the population from the surrounding working-class districts, and by council workers. U1 runs to Alte Donau on the river bank and the stop is near the Danube Park recreation area, the second largest park in Vienna.

Following further regulation, in 1972 the 21km long slither of the Donauinsel (Danube Island) was artificially created. It also offers bathing facilities and cycling or walking routes. U1 stops at Donauinsel, and there are several ferries for walkers and cyclists from the Prater side across to the island.

WIENERWALD

In the early 19th century the inhabitants of Europe discovered 'nature' as a romantically pleasurable idyll, not simply a source of discomfort and menace. For the Viennese, the focus of this new attitude was the Wienerwald (Vienna Woods); the Biedermeier painters began to highlight its charm on canvas, poets and composers meditated on it, family groups set off on Wienerwald excursions. Thus was the erstwhile haunt of bears and wolves, of outlaws and hermits, transformed and tamed.

Access to the Viennese woods for ramblers is possible from many branches of the public transport in the western purlieus of the city – for example from the end of Tram 49 at Hütteldorf, from Neuwaldegg and Salmannsdorf, and from Baden, reached by a tram direct from the Opera. The *Höhenstrasse* is a panoramic winding road along the edge of the woods. The Rathaus (City Hall) issues free leaflets showing rambling routes through the Wienerwald.

VIEWS OF VIENNA
In the city

The **Upper Belvedere** (see page 50) offers fine views of the city centre from the second-floor gallery.

The **Donauturm** in Donaupark has revolving restaurants/cafés on two levels, at 160m and 170m.

The **Gloriette** in Schönbrunn Park (see page 106) has views of the palace and west Vienna.

Haas Haus, opposite St Stephen's, has a café on the top floor with a good view of the cathedral.

The **Riesenrad** (big wheel) in the Prater (see page 98) is 67m high at the top. Open: April to September 9am–11pm; shortened hours in winter.

Autumn colours of the Wienerwald

St Stephen's South Tower (Steffl) has a viewing platform at 72m. Open: daily March to October 9am–5.30pm, November to February 9am–4.30pm. The **North Tower** (Adlerturm) has a lift to a look-out point at 60m. Open: daily 9am–5.30pm.

AROUND VIENNA

Bellevuehöhe

There was previously a hotel here, where Freud once stayed and wrote to his friend Wilhelm Fliess: 'Do you really think that one day a marble plaque will be fixed to this house with the words: "Here on 24 July 1895 the secret of dreams was revealed to Dr Sigmund Freud." The chances seem slim.' These words are now on a monument, from where there is a fine view of the city (see page 41).

The **Kahlenberg** (484m) and **Leopoldsberg** (425m) are reached with Bus 38A. From here was launched the final assault that drove off the Turks in 1683. Franz Grillparzer wrote: 'If you view from Kahlenberg the land, My writings and myself you'll understand.'

The two highest outlook points within the Wienerwald itself are the **Jubiläumswarte** (388m), one-and-a-half hours on foot from **Neuwaldegg**; and the **Habsburgerwarte** (542m) one-and-a-half hours from Grinzing.

Viennese Secession and Jugendstil

In the second half of the 19th century, in painting as in architecture, the prevailing Viennese style was historicism, a sometimes replica-like recreation of Gothic, Renaissance and baroque. The increasing sterility of this approach provoked a reaction all over Europe; a new, sensuous, flowing style was born, known as Art Nouveau in francophone lands and Jugendstil in German-speaking ones. The Vienna Secession was the local expression of this new impulse, and indeed brought it to the highest pitch of perfection.

In architecture Otto Wagner and Josef Hoffmann, in painting Gustav Klimt, and in applied art Koloman Moser were the leading exponents of the Secession which, however, also drew inspiration from the work of the Scot Charles Rennie Mackintosh. Secessionist works combined a pronounced sensuality (as in Klimt's openly erotic paintings) with an emphasis on

functionalism or 'truth to materials' (as in Otto Wagner's various public buildings). These two elements were not always pulling in the same direction. The *Wiener Werkstätte* began by aiming to make artefacts for all but ended by catering to a narrow and rich élite. In architecture, modernism as propagated by Adolf Loos went on to reject sensuality and opted for puritanical functional severity.

Wagner's Postparkassenamt, finished in 1912

The Majolka-Haus, by Otto Wagner

An inscription above the entrance to the Sezession

Karlsplatz Station, another of Wagner's masterpieces

Excursions to the West

KLOSTERNEUBURG

Some 13km upstream from Vienna is the ancient settlement of Klosterneuburg, now a dormitory town for well-to-do commuters, but once the spiritual and intellectual heart of Austria. The Margraves of Babenberg, who ruled the eastern marches of the German Empire before the advent of the Habsburgs, only gradually moved their administrative centre down the Danube to Vienna. After being established at Melk and Tulln they arrived at Klosterneuburg at the beginning of the 12th century.

According to legend, the veil of Lady Agnes, wife of Leopold III of Babenberg, was whipped away by the wind as they stood on the cliff overlooking the Danube where it landed was interpreted as where the pious Margrave should build a new monastery. Leopold put the work in hand and the building was consecrated in 1136. The monastery was occupied by the Augustine Canons, who made it the centre of learning for the whole of the Austrian Crown Lands; its library is still the most richly endowed of any monastery in the country with 160,000 volumes.

In the 18th century Charles VI commissioned Donato Felice d'Allio to draw up ambitious plans for Klosterneuburg. However, Charles died before much progress could be made.

In the Stiftskeller near the entrance, a festival is held each year on St Leopold's Day (15 November), with free wine tasting and 'barrel-sliding' inside a huge cask with a capacity of 56,000 litres. Not far away is the Chapel of St Sebastian, housing the so-called Albrecht Altarpiece (after Duke Albrecht of Habsburg – 1439). One of the panels shows the earliest extant view of Vienna.

The church and monastery tour

The two towers to the church were remodelled by Friedrich Schmidt in the 19th century, but were originally built in the 15th and 17th centuries. Inside there are a number of fine baroque frescos.

EXCURSIONS

Gföhl · Kamp
Lichtenau
Langenlois
Krems · Krems an der Donau
Dürnstein · Furth · Dona
Spitz · Traismau
Benediktinerstift Göttweig
Pöggstall · Burgruine Aggstein · Herzogenburg
Melk · St Pölten · Böheimkirch
Loosdorf
Ybbs-an-der-Donau · Schloss Schallaburg
St Leonhard · Traisen
Wieselburg · Mank
Purgstall · Wilhelmsburg
Pielach · Traisen · Hainfeld
Scheibbs · Kirchberg an der Pielach · Lilienfeld
▲ Reisalpe 1398m
Türnitz
Gaming · Erlauf
Ötscher ▲ 1893m · St Aegyd
Wallfahrtskirche
Mariazell · Mürzsteg
Kräuterin · Salza · Mürz
Mürzzuschlag

On a lower level is the cloister, the refectory and the St Leopold Chapel, with a cycle of frescos depicting the life of the saint. Behind an ornate grille is the greatest artistic treasure of the monastery, the *Verdun Altarpiece*. This is a reconstruction of the original (damaged by fire in the 14th century) which was made by Nicholas of Verdun in 1191. Its front consists of 45 beautifully worked enamelled plates, the most exquisite enamel work that has survived from the Middle Ages.

The tour continues with the baroque buildings designed by Donato Felice d'Allio, and the Treasury, which contains the crown of the Archdukes of Austria. The Grand or Imperial Staircase leads to the library and the Marble Hall with a ceiling fresco by Daniel Gran.

Reached by train from Franz-Josefs-Bahnhof or by bus from U1 in Heiligenstadt. Tours from 9am–noon and 1.30pm–dusk, providing there are enough people. Admission charge.

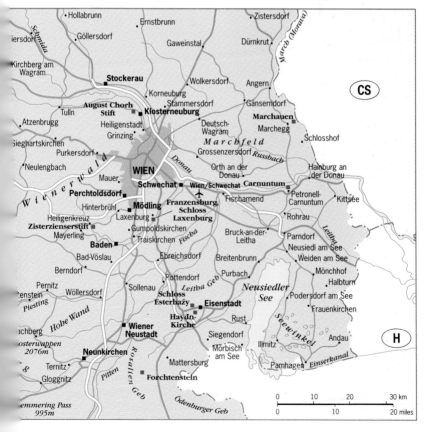

Excursions to the West

The ruined castle at Dürnstein provides a picturesque backdrop

'Kremser' Schmidt, Martino Altomonte and Franz Anton Maulbertsch. The Historical Museum is on Dominikanerplatz.

90km from Vienna, on Road 3. Trains from Franz-Josefs-Bahnhof. Tel: 02732–2511 ext 338–9. Open: April to October, Tuesday to Saturday 9am–noon, 2pm–5pm; Sundays 9am–noon. Admission charge.

DÜRNSTEIN

The ruined castle at Dürnstein once housed a famous prisoner, Richard Coeur-de-Lion (The Lionheart) of England. This unfortunate monarch insulted the Babenberg Duke and annoyed the German Emperor during the Third Crusade. On his way home he was arrested on the outskirts of Vienna and imprisoned, while negotiations proceeded for an enormous ransom. When this was paid, it financed new fortifications in Vienna and two other castles. The story about Richard's minstrel Blondel discovering him by singing outside the castle windows is fabrication. At the north end of the High Street is a splendid baroque monastery built by Matthias Steinl in the 18th century.

9km west of Krems. For information: tel: 02711–219.

KREMS AN DER DONAU

Where the Danube and the Krems rivers converge a fortress grew up in the 10th century, the outline of which is still extant. Krems is now merged with the similarly ancient riparian town of Stein, which is also worth visiting, although the high security prison for hard-case criminals is a lowering presence. In Krems the Parish Church of St Vitus on Pfarrplatz contains fine baroque frescos by

GÖTTWEIG

The great Benedictine abbey of Göttweig is situated on a commanding height 260m above the river and has an impressive view over the surrounding countryside. Known as Austria's answer to Monte Cassino, it is one of the loveliest of the great baroque cloisters along the Danube. The earlier part – the

choir of the monastery church – is late Gothic, with later baroque additions by Cypriano Biasino. The church's exuberantly decorated interior shimmers with blue and gold. Lukas von Hildebrandt was commissioned to reconstruct the buildings and to add noble courtyards in 1718, but the project was only partially carried through.
5km south of Krems. Tel: 02732–5582. Open: May to October, Tuesday, Friday to Sunday and holidays. Admission charge.

MELK

Melk is situated on the western edge of one of the most beautiful areas of Danubian landscape, namely the *Wachau*, famous for its vineyards and orchards. It is built on a rocky promontory affording breathtaking views of a southern arm of the Danube. The history of the monastery reaches back to Babenberg times, Melk having been the centre of their administration before they moved downstream to Tulln, Klosterneuburg and finally Vienna.

In the 15th century Melk was the centre of religious reform among the Benedictines of Austria and southern Germany. Spiritual renewal and the increase of learning were features of the contemplative life here as elsewhere. The monastery church was rebuilt more splendidly than before in 1429.

Under the Abbott Berthold Dietmayr in the 18th century, Jakob Prandtauer was commissioned to build what was to become his greatest achievement, a huge baroque monastery. He worked on it between 1701 and 1726, leaving the work unfinished on his death in that year.

The tour takes you through the courtyards, long corridors and noble rooms with stucco and frescos. The far

Melk's monastery dominates the Danube

end is an oval terrace, from where the view over the river can be admired. The library is entered next, followed by the church, which boasts one of the most glittering baroque interiors to be seen in Austria. The splendid high altar is the work of Antonio Beduzzi, with statues by Antonio Mattielli. Most of the frescos are by Johann Michael Rottmayr.
79km west of Vienna on the A1. Tel: 02752–2312. Guided tours: daily at 9am, 10am, 11am, 2pm, 3pm and 5pm. Sundays from 10am. Admission charge.

SCHLOSS SCHALLABURG

Parts of the romantic castle date to the 12th century (the keep) but it is primarily a product of the Renaissance, with a large inner courtyard flanked by magnificent arcades. Major exhibitions are frequently held here.
6km south of Melk. Admission charge.

Excursions to the South

Get away from it all in the beautiful Vienna Woods at Baden

BADEN

A fault in the earth's crust where the eastern edge of the Alps meets the flat land of the 'Vienna Basin' has produced an abundance of thermal springs along its course. These were exploited at Baden even in Roman times and Marcus Aurelius himself spoke approvingly of the 'Pannonian waters' here. They remained an attraction throughout the Middle Ages and the baroque period. Mozart's wife was continually 'taking the cure' – to which fact we probably owe the lovely *Ave verum* chorus written for Anton Stoll, the choirmaster of the parish church. (A plaque on the wall of the church recalls this commission.)

The heyday of Baden, however, was undoubtedly the early 19th century, when the Emperor Franz made it his summer residence. The town centre retains its Biedermeier character, a large number of buildings having been designed by the leading neoclassicist architect Joseph Kornhäusel. The substantial Sauerhof, formerly a hospital, was one of his most ambitious works.

The lovely Wienerwald

There are several baths in neoclassical buildings which are still operational, their sulphurous waters being efficacious against rheumatism. Kornhäusel built the City Hall and the so-called Florastöckl at Frauengasse no 5. There is also a pleasant park, a theatre and a casino, all exuding the atmosphere of a bygone age.

Reached by the Lokalbahn that runs from opposite the Opera to Josefsplatz in the centre of Baden.

GUMPOLDSKIRCHEN

Wine connoisseurs may well like to combine a trip to Baden with a visit to the charming village of Gumpoldskirchen, one of Austria's best-known centres of quality wine production. There are many *Heurige* in the village offering the speciality of the region: fruity, smooth white wines from the Zierfandler, Rotgipfler and Neuburger grapes.

Between Mödling and Baden, southwest of Vienna on Road 12.

HEILIGENKREUZ

The Cistercian monastery at Heiligenkreuz was founded by Leopold III of Babenberg in 1133, and was named after the True Cross, a fragment of which is preserved in the tabernacle of the main altar. The architecture is mostly austere and imposing as befits the Cistercian tradition. The soaring nave of the Gothic church is its most striking feature, the contrast between the dimly lit nave and the illumination of the great choir producing a remarkable sensation of spiritual elevation.

30km southwest of Vienna. Off Road 11. Guided tours: 8am–11am and 1.30pm–5.30pm every hour. Sundays 1.30pm–5.30pm. Admission charge.

The Trinity Pillar in Heiligenkreuz

MAYERLING

Deep in the Viennese Woods the Carmelite nuns at Mayerling pray continually for the soul of Crown Prince Rudolf, who committed suicide in the hunting lodge that formerly stood here. Before taking his own life, he killed his lover, Marie Vetsera. A few relics of the tragedy are exhibited near the sacristy of the chapel.

15km west of Heiligenkreuz.

PERCHTOLDSDORF

The most striking feature of this little village on the outskirts of the city is the massive tower of 1465 and the Gothic church next to it, which dates to the mid-14th century. When the Turks approached Vienna in 1683 the population of Perchtoldsdorf took refuge in the church. After negotiating a ransom with the invaders, they emerged, expecting to be allowed to return to their houses, but were massacred to a man. Near the town hall is an impressive plague column, a less elaborate version of the one on the Graben, but also designed by Fischer von Erlach.

Exit from Southern Motorway at Brunn am Gebirge.

Excursions to the South

LAXENBURG

The earliest imperial connection with Laxenburg goes back to the reign of Albert the Lame of Habsburg (1330–1358) and his son Albert III. Between them they acquired a hunting reserve near the village of the same name and some buildings formerly belonging to the monastery at Melk. A castle was built in 1381, later altered by the court architect Ludovico Burnacini, after the Turkish siege. This much restored edifice now houses the Austrian Film Archives.

The so-called New Castle or Blauer Hof was built by the architect of Schönbrunn, Nikolaus Pacassi. It was here that one of the archdukes with a passion for fireworks was killed by an exploding rocket during a show he laid on for Emperor Franz II and his new Empress in 1795. The same Emperor Franz built the most spectacular of the surviving sights of Laxenburg, a fake medieval castle known as the Franzensburg. Surrounded by a large moat, with islands and bridges and a magnificent park, this architectural eccentricity by Michael Riedl and Franz Jäger is the most striking example of Romanticism in early-19th-century Austria. Recently it has been carefully restored and is again open to the public. Highlights are the 'Habsburg Hall' with 17 marble statues of the Dukes and Emperors up to the time of Maria Theresa, the Throne Room, the Chapel and the Lorraine Hall. There is also an all too realistic re-creation of a medieval dungeon, complete with an imprisoned 'knight'.

In Laxenburg one has a glimpse of the private world of the Habsburgs at play or basking in the rays of their dynastic myth. The last Emperor, Charles I, lived periodically in the New Castle between 1916 and 1918 and received Kaiser Wilhelm of Germany here shortly before the overthrow of their respective dynasties.

15km south of Vienna, off the Southern Motorway. Reached by bus from Landstrasse (U3, U4) or Südtirolerplatz (U1). Open: Easter to end October, daily 8am–6pm (Franzensburg). Guided groups only. Admission charge.

Boating on Franzensburg's moat

Excursions to the East

CARNUNTUM–PETRONELL

Carnuntum was the main Roman garrison for Pannonia, *Vindobona* (Vienna) being subsidiary to it. There is a 2nd-century Roman amphitheatre, and south of it an impressive Heidentor, thought to have been a triumphal arch. Near by is Schloss Traun with a small museum devoted to the Natural History of the Danube.

41km east of Vienna, beyond Schwechat airport on Road 9. Museum open: April to November, daily except Mondays 10am–5pm.

ROHRAU

In the village is the birthplace of Joseph Haydn, now a museum. To the south is Schloss Rohrau, principal residence of the Harrachs. Their picture collection was moved here from their palace on Freyung in Vienna (now sold). It has a large number of works by Italian, Flemish, Spanish and other artists.

6km south of Carnuntum/Petronell on Road 211. Haydn Museum – open: daily, except Mondays, 10am–5pm. Admission charge. Schloss Rohrau – open: April to October, daily except Mondays 10am–5pm. Admission charge.

NEUSIEDLER SEE

Known as the 'Sea of the Viennese', the Neusiedler See offers aquatic sports (especially windsurfing) in a picturesque nature reserve. Around the shores some of the best wine in Austria is made and can be sampled in charming villages such as Rust, Mörbisch and Purbach. North-east of the latter is the Schlossmuseum Halbturn, where specialised exhibitions of the Austrian Gallery in the Belvedere

Windsurfers' paradise at Neusiedler See

are staged. There is a pleasant pub in the courtyard of the Schloss.

50km southeast of Vienna on Road 10, 70km on Road 16. Schlossmuseum Halbturn – tel: 02172/2237 or 8577. Open: May to October, daily 9.30am–5pm.

EISENSTADT

The main sights are: the Esterhazy Palace (with the Haydn room).

52km southeast of Vienna on Road 16. Tel: 02682/3384. Open: June to September 9am–5pm; October to May 10am–4pm. English guided tours every half hour July to September, every hour October to June. Admission charge.

Haydn's House

Tel: 02682/5040. Open: 10am–5pm, weekends 10am–4pm.

The Calvary Hill and Haydn Mausoleum

Open: daily 9am–5pm.

Shopping

Most people who go shopping in Vienna will be on the look-out for something specifically Viennese, or at least Austrian, even though they can, if they wish, buy a sweater from Pringle of Scotland on the Kohlmarkt or Earl Grey tea from Schönbichler on the Wollzeile. Broadly speaking, the most popular items will be those which continue or tastefully re-create the great traditions of Viennese design – costume jewellery, ornaments and textiles that recall the achievements of the Wiener Werkstätte and the Secession at the turn of the century, or paper designs and objects that derive their inspiration from the early-19th-century Biedermeier period; or glass, whose neo-baroque or neo-Renaissance lustre reflects the mid-19th-century passion for Historicism; or porcelain from the Augarten factory firm that was founded in the 18th century.

More generally 'Austrian' are the famous green Loden coats made of pressed felt, and the *Tracht*, a costume that has its origin in folk dress (it does not really travel however).

The prestige shopping area of the city is in the pedestrian zone making three sides of a rectangle – Kohlmarkt, Graben and Kärntner Strasse, although there are certainly numerous high-quality shops in other parts of the Inner City. The main shopping street with department stores is the Mariahilfer Strasse, nicknamed Magyarhilfer Strasse in the late 1980s because of the huge influx of Hungarian shoppers, hungry for consumer goods and computers. Here are the two great stores Herzmansky and Gerngross, although Vienna was never really a city of mega-stores.

Two other long streets also offer shopping opportunities to suit those with a more modest pocket: Favoritenstrasse and Landstrasse. Arcades with specialised smaller shops are few and far between but there is an attractive one running through the Ferstel Palais and an alley with shops behind St Michael's Church.

First–class shopping: candles on display in the Kohlmarkt

Practical Tips

In most of the larger establishments, and all of those with a big turnover from tourism, there will be assistants who speak good English. Although the situation has somewhat improved in recent years, there is still a tendency to discourage browsing; few people can convey a mixture of brittle impatience and ill-concealed disgust with the ditherer or non-puchaser than one or two of the assistants in expensive Viennese shops. Furthermore, there is usually no truck with the practice of exchanging or returning goods (unless they are faulty). Until recently, there were regulations restricting an individual shop owner's right to stage a sale or drop prices, and opening hours are still controlled by law (not with the consumer's interest in mind), although there has been some relaxation. An awareness of such aspects of the retail culture will help you to get the best out of your shopping.

Normal opening hours for shops are as follows: Monday to Friday,

Fruit-sellers in the Naschmarkt

Lobmeyr Glass Shop, Kärtner Strasse

8am–6.30pm (foodshops are often open from 7am); Saturday, 8am–1pm. Many shops close for two hours at midday. Shops may choose one evening in the week for late opening, or remain open all day on the first Saturday of the month (9am–5pm). Stores and supermarkets usually choose this option. All shops are open all day the last two (so-called Silver and Gold) Saturdays before Christmas. Shops in the Westbahnhof and the Südbahnhof are open from 7am–11pm.

Value Added Tax (*Mehrwertsteuer*) at 20 per cent is levied on most goods and a few also have a luxury tax. VAT may be reclaimed on exporting the article if you fill in a form (U34) supplied by the shop (many retailers display a 'Tax Free for Tourists' sign). The form must be stamped by the customs at the point of exit from the country, if the VAT element is to be reclaimed. This can either be done by post or directly at most exchange offices and banks on the border crossing.

Shopping

TRADITIONAL AUSTRIAN CLOTHING

Eduard Kettner
Seilergasse 12. Tel: 513 22 39.
Loden-Plankl.
Michaelerplatz 6. Tel: 533 80 32.
Wantky
Tuchlauben 18. Tel: 63 05 53.
Witzky
Stephansplatz 7. Tel: 512 48 43.

OTHER CLOTHING SHOPS

Ladies Fashions and Casual Wear

Alexander
Rauhensteingasse 10. Tel: 512 39 46.
Eisenbaul
Plankengasse 4. Tel: 512 28 91.
Haider-Petkov
Kohlmarkt 11. Tel: 533 20 05.
Knize
Graben 13. Tel: 512 21 19.

Menswear

Adonis
Kohlmarkt 11. Tel: 533 70 35.
Alexander
Rauhensteingasse 10. Tel: 512 39 46.

LEATHERS AND FURS

Foggensteiner
Rathausstrasse 15. Tel: 43 08 17.
Liska
Kärntner Strasse 8. Tel: 512 41 20.
Mossboek
Gumpendorfer Strasse 56. Tel: 586 13 43.
Popp und Kretschmer
Kärntner Strasse 51. Tel: 512 64 21.

LEATHER GOODS

Hans Novotny
Reasonably priced leather goods made in the Novotnys' own workshop.
Spiegelgasse 6. Tel: 512 23 36.

SHOES

Zak
Kärntner Strasse 36. Tel: 512 72 57.

JEWELLERY, WATCHES AND CLOCKS

Haban
Kärntner Strasse 2. Tel: 512 67 30–0.
Heldwein
Graben 13. Tel: 512 57 81.
Hübner
Graben 28. Tel: 533 80 65.
A E Köchert
Neuer Markt 15. Tel: 512 58 28.

SPECTACLES

Schau-Schau
If you are looking for something outrageous, elegant or simply unusual in spectacles-design, this may be the place for you.
Rotenturmstrasse 11, corner of Ertlgasse. Tel: 533 45 84.

BOOKS

Books in English are formidably expensive in Vienna.

The British Bookshop
Carries a good stock of British paperbacks.
Weihburggasse 8. Tel: 512 19 45.
Frick
On the first floor, books in English and other languages. Good selection of books about Vienna/Austria.
Graben 27. Tel: 533 99 14.
Georg Prachner
The best stock of more specialised books

in various languages on Vienna's art and architecture.
Kärntner Strasse 30. Tel: 512 85 49.

Shakespeare & Co
The only shop carrying a substantial number of American books. There is also a good literary paperback selection.
Sterngasse 2. Tel: 535 50 53.

RECORDS, CASSETTES AND COMPACT DISCS

Carola
Albertinapassage (ie in the underpass). Tel: 56 41 14.

Columbia
Kärntner Strasse 30. Tel: 512 36 75

Schallplatten-Wiege am Graben
Graben 29a. Tel: 533 20 32.

VIENNESE DESIGN AND ARTEFACTS

In the Centre

Augarten Porcelain Factory
Elegant porcelain from Austria's long-established producer.
Stock-im-Eisen-Platz 3–4. Tel: 512 14 94.

Joh Backhausen & Söhne
The original producers for the Wiener Werkstätte (whose pattern books they retain) offer a large selection of textiles and fabrics to WW designs.
Kärntner Strasse 33. Tel: 514 04.

Baumgartner am Graben
Writing paper and accoutrements with a Biedermeier flavour.
Graben 12. Tel: 512 62 43.

Bösendorfer
Famous piano makers – so famous the street is named after them!
Bösendorferstrasse 12. Tel: 505 35 18.

Cecconi
Woodcarving.
Stephansplatz 4. Tel: 513 72 22.

Delarue
Petit point.
Seilergasse 3. Tel: 512 82 79.

Josef Kober
Souvenirs, tin soldiers and toys.
Graben 14–15. Tel: 533 60 18.

Lobmeyr
Historicist glassware, porcelain, lamps, from the famous firm founded in 1823.
Kärntner Strasse 26. Tel: 512 05 08.

Österreichische Werkstätten
Ornamental objects, costume jewellery, handicrafts.
Kärntner Strasse 26. Tel: 512 24 18.

Smejkal
Petit point.
Opernpassage. Tel: 587 21 02.

Thonet
Bent-wood furniture.
Kohlmarkt 6. Tel: 63 77 88.

Outside the city centre

Porzellanmanufaktur, Augarten
Obere Augartenstrasse. Tel: 211 24.

Wiener Emailmanufaktur Michaela Frey Team
Enamel Work.
Gumpendorfer Strasse 81. Tel: 597 11 60.

Fuhrmann
Viennese bronzes.
Stolzenthalergasse 8. Tel: 42 43 93.

Wiener Keramikmanufaktur
Ceramics.
Mariahilfer Strasse 164. Tel: 835 86 03.

Traditional Austrian costume

SHOPPING

Browsing in Kärtner Strasse

ANTIQUES

The big event in the year for the antiques trade is the *Wiener Antiquitäten Messe* (Antiques Fair) which takes place usually in the second and third weeks of November. The main part of this is held in the palatial surroundings of the Neue Hofburg, but in recent years it has spread out into the Ferstel Palais (Freyung 2) and the Palais Palffy (Josefsplatz 6). One of the bonuses for visitors (admission charge at each venue) is a rare chance to see the interiors of these locations (Ferstel's elaborately ornate upper chamber originally designed to house the stock exchange is particularly impressive). The most interesting items on display tend to be furniture and clocks although there is a large selection of over-priced pictures as well.

Dorotheum

This auction house is a great national institution, originally founded by Emperor Joseph I as a regulated pawn shop to protect citizens from rapacious money lenders. It was also the information centre for all matters concerning trading and the law.

The Dorotheum sells anything from junk to good-quality antiques. You can wander in any day and inspect the items coming up for auction in the next few weeks, all of them labelled with a reserve price. It is possible to pay an agent to bid for you – advisable if you are a non-German speaker, especially since the items are auctioned from their number tag and not on display as you bid. It is also possible to purchase some things direct from the display rooms. VAT is levied on the sale price and transport of goods can be arranged at an office on the top floor.

MARKETS

The *Flohmarkt* (Flea Market) occupies the southern end of the Naschmarkt (Linke Wienzeile) every Saturday except public holidays, 8am–6pm (U4 to Kettenbrückengasse). In the summer months there is an Antiques Market near Schwedenplatz at weekends (Saturday 2pm–8pm, Sunday 10am–8pm).

GALLERIES/DEALERS

Galleries and antique dealers have proliferated in the area around the Dorotheum (between Spiegelgasse and Bräunerstrasse). In these shops antique furniture, fine art, antiquarian books, prints and maps, together with *objets d'art* and jewellery are all to be found.

Alt Wien Kunst
Bräunerstrasse 11. Tel: 512 91 43.
Galerie Asboth
Asiatic art.
Spiegelgasse 19. Tel: 512 51 37.

Belle etage
Jugendstil artefacts.
Mahlerstrasse 15. Tel: 512 23 79.

D & J
Perhaps the most wide-ranging stock of antique clocks in the city, including empire, Biedermeier and neoclassical examples of great elegance.
Plankengasse 6. Tel: 512 29 72.

Hofstätter
Paintings and sculpture.
Bräunerstrasse 12. Tel: 533 50 70.

Glasgalerie Kovacek
Glass vases from 1600 to 1930, Bohemian hunting tankards, Tiffany vases and Historicist goblets. A speciality are their 19th-century French paperweights.
Stallburggasse 2. Tel: 512 99 54.

Christian Nebehay
Mr Nebehay is an expert on the Secession and the early Expressionists in Austria and has written a couple of helpful guidebooks for the visitor on these topics (usually available in Prachner on Kärntner Strasse).
Annagasse 18. Tel: 512 18 01.

Axel Peters
Jugendstil artefacts.
Siebensterngasse 24. Tel: 93 13 44.

Galerie Rauhenstein
Antique jewellery and other *objets d'art.*
Rauhensteingasse 3. Tel: 513 33 09.

Sonja Reisch
A treasure-trove of Biedermeier.
Stallburggasse 4. Tel: 535 52 15.

Szaal
Also Biedermeier.
Josefstädter Strasse 74. Tel: 42 65 41.

20th Century
Furniture, design and decorative art from Jugendstil to post-modern. Interesting for art deco fans and those interested in 1950s design.

Bauernmarkt 9. Tel: 63 72 22.
Galerie Walfischgasse
Jugendstil.
Walfischgasse 12. Tel: 512 37 16.

Wiener Interieur
Dorotheergasse 14. Tel: 512 28 98.

Ingrid Zerunian
An immensely knowledgeable gallery owner, who will help look for specific objects, and arrange for their restoration.
Piaristengasse 18. Tel: 431 92 22.

ANTIQUARIAN BOOKS AND PRINTS

Altbuchdienst
Books, postcards, records.
Dr-Karl-Lueger-Platz 3. Tel: 512 64 00.

Wolfrum
This conveniently placed bookshop near the Augustinerkirche has a large selection of reproductions by Austrian artists, as well as views, prints and a good stock of art books.
Augustinerstrasse 10. Tel: 512 53 98.

Viennese petit point embroidery

Entertainment

The Burgtheater's staircase, with ceiling frescos by the Klimt brothers

THEATRE

The writer, Jörg Mauthe, has remarked that, for the Viennese, 'music and theatre are not abstract phenomena, worshipped from afar and in practice only important for intellectuals and the social élite. They are vital to the lives of the inhabitants and follow immediately after eating and drinking in importance and are way ahead of sex.' Anyone who spends time in the capital will become aware of the truth of this remark – new productions are front page news here and informed opinion is not the exclusive province of the self-styled aficionado.

There must be spectacles!

The passion for the theatre goes back to baroque times when the Habsburgs and the nobility laid on lavish entertainments - 'there must be spectacles' decreed Maria Theresa, 'a city needs that.' At the same time the Jesuits, who were the motor of the Counter-Reformation in Austria, recognised the didactic value of visual and theatrical display. In the 19th century an actor like Girardi mirrored the different orders of Viennese society, and was in turn imitated by his delighted public. 'We are always play-acting,' observed the playwright Arthur Schnitzler sourly, 'the clever man understands that.' The Burgtheater, a national institution with a tradition going back two centuries, was for a long time a model for refined speech and its players had a distinctive mode of expression.

All the theatres in Vienna receive a subsidy. The fare they offer ranges from classics of the German and European theatre (mostly in the Burgtheater and the Volkstheater) to productions of modern dramatists (many of them British or American) and fringe or experimental works, often held in locations like cellars or cafés. The great Viennese dramatists – Johann Nestroy, Ferdinand Raimund, Franz Grillparzer – are little known in the English-speaking world, because of a scarcity of translations. (However, Thornton Wilder's adaptation of a Nestroy piece ended up as the blockbusting musical *Hello Dolly*.) German speakers should therefore seize the chance to sample Viennese works.

The Burgtheater

The most celebrated theatre in Vienna is the Burgtheater. In recent years it has had a dynamic German director (Claus Peymann) and provoked scandals and uproar by staging Thomas Bernhard's bitter attack on his countrymen's complacency in Heldenplatz in 1988 (see page 22).
Dr-Karl-Lueger-Ring 2. Tel: 514 44 2959.

The **Volkstheater** *(Neustiftgasse 1, tel: 93 27 76)*, the **Theater in der Josefstadt** *(Josefstädter Strasse 24–26, tel: 402 51 27)*, the **Kammerspiele** *(Rotenturmstrasse 2, tel: 533 28 33)* and the **Akademietheater** *(Lisztstrasse 1, tel: 514 44 2959)* – an alternative stage for the Burgtheater company – offer the full range of classical and modern drama, Viennese or foreign.

The **Raimundtheater** *(Wallgasse 18–20, tel: 59 97 70)*, the **Theater an der Wien** *(Linke Wienzeile 6, tel: 588 30 237)* and the **Ronacher** *(Himmelpfortgasse 25, tel: 513 83 40)* are the musical theatres, the former having had a record-breaking run with *Cats* and followed by a

musical based on the life and work of Sigmund Freud.

Of particular interest to those constrained by the language barrier is the superb **Serapionstheater** *(Taborstrasse 10, tel: 24 55 62)*, whose brilliant company perform a wordless show of mime, dance and tableaux.

Theater in der Josefstadt

There is open-air theatre between May and September – revues at the **Hernalser Stadttheater** *(Geblergasse 50, tel: 43 35 43)*, folk and improvisation theatre at the **Original Wiener Stegreifbühne** *(Maroltingergasse 43, tel: 92 46 05)* and classic Austrian drama at the **Jura Soyfer Theater am Spittelberg** *(Spittelberggasse 7–10, tel: 93 24 58-0)*.

Regular performances in English take place at two locales, Vienna's **English Theatre** *(Josefsgasse 12, tel: 402 12 60)* and the **International Theatre** *(Porzellangasse, Corner Müllnergasse, tel: 31 62 72)*. The former sometimes features guest appearances by well-known actors and actresses. (For information about theatre booking generally, see page 184).

ENTERTAINMENT

FRINGE THEATRE, CABARET, FLOOR SHOWS

Vienna has a long tradition of cabaret, much of it scathingly political. The best fringe theatre and cabaret performances are on offer from **Theater Gruppe 80** *(Gumpendorfer Strasse 67, tel: 56 52 22)*, **Theater Kabarett Simpl** *(Wollzeile 36, tel: 512 47 42)* – hosting many famous names of Viennese satire, **Freie Bühne Wieden** *(Wiedner Hauptstrasse 60b, tel: 586 21 22)*, **Metropol** *(Hernalser Hauptstrasse 55, tel: 43 35 43)*, **Kabarett Niedermair** *(Lenaugasse 1a, tel: 48 44 92)*, and **Spektakel** *(Hamburgerstrasse 14, tel: 587 06 23)*. Floor shows are not a Viennese speciality, but there are a few establishments, such as the **Casanova Revue-Bar Theater** *(Dorotheergasse 6-8, tel: 512 98 45)*, **Eden-Bar** *(Liliengasse 2, tel: 512 74 50)* or the **Moulin Rouge** *(Walfischgasse 11, tel: 512 130)*, which offer something glamorous, but at a price.

The bright lights of Vienna by night

JAZZ

Vienna has an extremely vivid jazz scene encompassing the whole range of the genre and frequently enlivened with guest appearances by international stars. Venues include the **Alte Schmiede** *(Schönlaterngasse 9, tel: 512 83 29)*, the **Bösendorfer-Saal** *(Graf-Starhemberg-Gasse 14, tel: 65 66 51)*, the **Dixieland Club** *(Wiedner Hauptstrasse 130, tel: 54 43 09)*, **Duke's** *(Gumpendorfer Strasse 9, tel: 56 86 29)*, **Jazzland** *(Franz-Josefs-Kai 29, tel: 533 25 75)*, **Miles Smiles** *(Lange Gasse 51, tel: 42 84 814)*, **Jazz-Spelunke** *(Dürergasse 3, tel: 587 01 26)* and **Opus One** *(Mahlerstrasse 11, tel: 513 20 75)*. These establishments are generally open into the early hours. The performers on the current programme of the more important locales are listed in the monthly programme of events obtainable from the Tourist Information Office.

OTHER MUSIC VENUES

Papas Tapas *(Schwarzenbergplatz 10, tel: 65 03 11)* is one of the few places in Vienna offering country music, together

with **Nashville** *(Siebenbrunnengasse 5a, tel: 55 73 89)*, which has live performances twice a week.

Rockhaus *(Adalbert-Stifter-Strasse 73, tel: 33 46 41)* is, as the name suggests, a rock'n'roll sanctuary.

At **America Latina** *(Mollardgasse 17, tel: 597 32 69)*, **Arauco** *(Krummgasse 1a, tel: 73 48 532)* and **Rincon Andino** *(Münzwardeingasse 2, tel: 587 61 25)* Latin American music is played by locals or visiting stars.

THE SCENE

The focal point of the Viennese scene is the so-called Bermuda Triangle, a tangle of narrowish streets south of Schwedenplatz – Rabensteig, Seitenstettengasse, Judengasse and others. A number of establishments regularly sink without trace, but others have showed considerable staying power – small *Beisls*, cafés and bars with live music or some alcoholic or gastronomic speciality to offer. With a few exceptions, places listed below are in or near the Bermuda Triangle.

Alt Wien Watering hole for artists and would-be Bohemians. *Bäckerstrasse 9. Tel: 52 52 22. Open: 10am–2am.*
Lukas Drinkers' paradise with huge choice of beverages. *Schönlaterngasse 2. Tel: 513 50 90. Open: till 2am, Friday and Saturday till 4am.*
Mardi Gras Music and cocktails. *Seilergasse 1. Tel: 52 67 63. Open: till 4am, Sundays till 1am.*
Roter Engel Chansons and cabaret; good wines. Always crowded. *Rabensteig /Seitenstettengasse 5. Tel: 535 41 05. Open: till 4am.*
Tunnel Three floors with a choice of

music, art shows or literary workshop. *Florianigasse 39. Tel: 42 34 65. In the Josefstadt.*

DISCOTHÈQUES/DANCING

There is now a large choice; three of the most well-known places are **P1** *(Rotgasse 3, tel: 535 99 95)* with spectacular lighting effects, **Café Splendide** *(Jasomirgottstrasse 3, tel: 533 34 30 –* exclusive dance locale, and the fashionable **U4** *(Schönbrunner Strasse 222, tel: 85 83 13)* with music videos.

Live music, Viennese style

CINEMA

Films in English are shown at the **Burg Kino** *(Opernring 19, tel: 587 84 06)*, the **De France** *(Schottenring 5, tel 34 52 36)*, and the **Star Kino** *(Burggasse 71, tel: 93 46 83)*. The **Austrian Film Museum** *(Augustinerstrasse 1, tel: 533 70 54 –* membership immediately on payment of a small fee) offers marvellous retrospectives of major or specialised film-makers in English and other languages.

Vienna in Myth and Cliché

Vienna conjures up images of Sacher Torte, waltzes, the Habsburgs as benign *pater patrias* and the romantic Blue Danube. Like all beguiling clichés these images are partly a reflection of reality and partly an evasion of it. The same goes for the received version of Viennese mores. From the early Middle Ages, clerics and other moralists had complained of the easy-going attitudes of the inhabitants, particularly with regard to wine, women and song. The great German dramatist, Friedrich Schiller, even wrote a poem in which he compared the Viennese to the Phaeacians of the *Odyssey*, a famously gluttonous people.

The Swabian preacher of the 17th century, Abraham a Sancta Clara, chastised them for their devotion to earthly pleasures and tried to threaten them with hellfire if they didn't behave as the church thought proper. A general impression of luxury, licentiousness, and idleness has thus pursued the Viennese through history; but the other side to this coin is the oft-described caution and scepticism of the burghers, their reputed meanness, petty-mindedness, hypocrisy and parochial respectability. The 'golden Viennese heart' is much in evidence, especially in tourist brochures, but residents know the backbiting and malice that has achieved the status of an art form in a city full of mordant wits.

The Habsburgs were mostly not benign, and the Danube is seldom, if ever, blue – but this is of little consequence. Their attributes are sanctified by tradition, or, as one writer put it: 'The Viennese eulogise the so-called good old days not because they love them so much, but because they so dislike the present.'

Staatsoper: one of the world's greatest opera houses

The Staatsoper opened in 1869 with Mozart's Don Giovanni

Vienna is a city obsessed with music

The opera house was built in early French Renaissance style

Classical and Sacred Music in Vienna

OPERA

There is an operatic tradition in Vienna that is almost as venerable as that of Italy, and indeed the early musical scene was dominated by Italian composers and librettists. Their works were lavish spectacles, often of an allegorical nature, not infrequently incorporating unblushing eulogy of the ruling house, which was their principal sponsor. In the 18th century, the Italian grip on opera was broken by the new German and Austrian composers, who insisted on more naturalistic plots and a closer integration of action, words and music.

When Christoph Willibald Gluck's marvellous *Orpheus and Euridice* was first performed in Vienna in 1762, to great applause, the court poet Metastasio left the theatre shaking his head – he knew his type of opera was doomed. The Italian tradition did not immediately die out, of course; as we have recently been reminded by Peter Shaffer's play, Mozart's great rival was Antonio Salieri, who composed no less than 40 operas. It is Mozart's works that have survived however, and one of them, The *Magic Flute,* has come to be regarded as the quintessentially 'Viennese' opera of the period, brilliantly combining joy and tragedy, high seriousness and low farce, with some of the loveliest music ever written for opera.

The Staatsoper (State Opera House) remains one of the premier opera houses in the world, inevitably with prices to match.
Opernring 1. Tel: 514 44/2960/2655.
The exception is the *Stehplätze,*

standing room tickets, that cost the equivalent of a couple of pounds and offer an unimpeded view of the stage from the back of the stalls. Queuing usually begins a couple of hours before the performance on the Operngasse side of the opera.

Staatsoper: a Viennese institution

The Volksoper is considerably cheaper, but not only for that reason to be recommended. Up and coming producers and an enthusiastic young company have recently provided some memorable operatic experiences. Don't miss their version of *Don Giovanni. Währinger Strasse 78. Tel: 514 44/3318/ 2657.*

The long tradition of music in Vienna had originally centred on the court and a number of Habsburg emperors had themselves been gifted executants and (not always so gifted) composers. At the beginning of the 19th century, the

The Vienna Boys' Choir conducts a sung mass on Sundays and Holy Days

increasingly autonomous musical life of the Viennese middle classes was reflected in the founding of the Society for the Friends of Music (still under imperial patronage). Its hall on Tuchlauben was soon perceived to be inadequate and a new building (see page 35) was eventually built between 1867 and 1869 to plans by Theophil von Hansen – the Musikverein. This is truly a musical shrine offering a rich programme of symphonic concerts and (in the smaller Brahms hall) chamber music throughout the year. It is the venue for the famous New Year's Day Concert of the Vienna Philharmonic of typical Viennese items, which is broadcast all over the world. *Karlsplatz 6. Tel: 65 81 90. Lothringerstrasse 20. Tel: 712 12 11.*

If the opportunity arises, it is worth going to chamber concerts in the baroque palaces (for example, the Schwarzenberg-Palais; Haydn concerts are held in the Esterházy-Palais and Beethoven concerts in the Lobkowitz–Palais). In October there is a programme of Strauss music in the Ferstel Palais.

The Vienna Boys' Choir performs a sung mass in the Burgkapelle (Hofburg, Schweizerhof – Sundays, September to June, 9.15am, postal booking: Hofmusik-kapelle, Hofburg, A-1010 Vienna). The Augustinerkirche has sung masses on Sunday mornings – details from the monthly events programmes obtainable from the Tourist Information Bureau.

Reisen and Freizeit, the Thomas Cook representative at Mariahilferstrasse 20 can provide programmes and make reservations for all events such as theatre tickets, opera tickets, concerts and sightseeing tours.

VIENNA BOYS' CHOIR

The Vienna Boys' Choir was founded in 1498 by Emperor Maximilian I and subsequently saw the beginning of many extremely successful Viennese careers. Its alumni included Joseph Haydn, Franz Schubert, Hans Richter and Clemens Krauss, to name but a few. It has proved even to be a good start in life for others who went on to conquer diverse realms outside the musical profession.

Sightseeing Tours

*D*epending on the time available, visitors may want a quick impression of the city from the window of a bus, a leisurely trundle round in a fiaker or a tram, a view from the river or even one from the air! All are available for the eager sightseer in the high season, and most of them throughout the year.

Sightseeing in style

A standard bus tour is offered by **Vienna Sightseeing Tours,** *(Stelzhamergasse 4, tel: 712 46 83)*. Fiakers can be picked up in summer in the Heldenplatz, the Albertinaplatz and beside the Stephansdom – fix the length of your tour and the price with the driver before you set off. A speciality of Vienna is the Oldtimer Tramway tour from Karlsplatz on holidays and at weekends from May to September (Saturday 1.30pm, Sunday and holidays 10am and 1.30pm – tel:

587 31 86 for information).

Boat trips (3 hours, 3 times daily from April to October, dance evenings Thursday, Friday and Saturday, *tel: 21750-451* for information) are available from the famous **Danubian Steamship Company** (DDSG). In the summer months there are skylark trips out of Schwechat airport (*tel: 67 94 54* for information, or travel agencies can also supply details of other tours on offer).

Interesting excursions are offered by **Cityrama Sightseeing Tours:** they include day and half-day trips that take in favourite sights such as the Spanish Riding School, Schönbrunn and Mayerling. The DDSG also offers river trips upstream to the Wachau and downstream to Bratislava. Individual guides are available from the **Vienna Guide Service** *(Sommerhaidenweg 124, tel: 44 30 940)* or **Travel Point Vienna** *(Boltzmanngasse 19, tel: 31 42 43)*.

For those who want more specific or recherché guidings relating to the infrastructure of Vienna, the City Hall organises a number of such: *tel: 40 00-81 0 50* for information from the **Rundfahrtenbüro Rathaus** – tickets available 2 weeks in advance. Similarly **Alternative Stadtrundfahrten** *(tel: 34 33 84)* offer something out of the mainstream.

City Bus: easy way to see the sights

THEME WALKS

An original idea of the city council was to institute a series of theme walks covering different aspects of Vienna's history, culture and architecture. They are extremely varied, and also take account of typical events, anniversaries, major exhibitions and so forth. A leaflet can be picked up from the Tourist Information Bureau at the southern end of Kärntner Strasse (no 38). Examples of the themes are: 'Old Houses, Tranquil Courtyards', 'On the Trail of the *Third Man*' and 'Unknown Vienna below Ground'. The brochure indicates whether any particular tour is offered in English (around half of the 30 or so available are); each walk lasts about $1\frac{1}{2}$ hours and costs about 100 Schillings, (reduced prices for young people).

BICYCLING

Route information is available from **Vienna Bike**, *(tel: 31 12 58.)*

FESTIVALS

Advance information about the annual festivals in Vienna may be obtained from the **Wiener Fremdenverkehrsverband**, *Obere Augartenstrasse 40, A-1025 Wien (tel: 222/211 14-0, fax 216 84 92)* and

brochures of the programmes are available from Tourist Information Offices and Travel Agencies during the relevant periods.

The Wiener Festwochen runs from mid-May to mid-June. The festival is built (approximately) around a central and topical theme (in 1990 it was 'Open Borders', in 1991 'Mozart'); it is deliberately designed to appeal to all levels of brow and consists of a mix of theatrical and musical productions and other events or exhibitions.

The Viennale Filmfestival takes place in March and April.

Traditional popular holidays with various events and activities are the Vienna Town Festival on 1 May, and the Donauinselfest at the end of May.

From July to September is the period of the Viennese Musical Summer with a number of special performances.

Take advantage of the trams

Children

*F*or many years the demographic profile of Vienna showed an ageing population, many of whom exhibited an almost legendary hostility to noisy children on public transport and in the streets. Although the apparent belief of some of the elderly Viennese that children should be seen and not heard (or preferably neither seen nor heard) still lingers on, Vienna is now considerably more child-friendly than it once was. The city council has exerted itself to create play areas in parts of the city lacking amenities for the young, and there is a substantial cultural programme for children throughout the year, although, of course, visitors will be excluded from some of this by the language barrier.

For general information on activities and events for young people (but primarily teenagers), as well as the pre-booking of tickets, apply to **Jugend in Wien** (Bellariapassage, open: Monday to Friday noon–7pm and Saturday 10am –7pm, tel: 526 46 37).

Street theatre for children

THEATRE FOR CHILDREN

Theatres offering shows where language is less of a problem, since animated puppets or mime supply most of the action, include the following:

Domino, Schwarzes Theater Silhouetten, Nesher Puppentheater
Sonnenfelsgasse 3/2b. Tel: 512 24 99.

Puppentheater Lilarum
Phillippsgasse 8. Tel: 89 42 103.

Urania Puppenspiele (Hans Kraus Theater)
Uraniastrasse 1. Tel: 72 61 91-0.

Serapionstheater im Odeon
Taborstrasse 10. Tel: 24 55 62 (see page 147).

Theatre for children in German is supplied by:

Märchenbühne 'Der Apfelbaum'
Burggasse 28-32. Tel: 93 17 29.

Metropolino
Shows for young people during carnival.
Hernalser Hauptstrasse 55. Tel: 43 35 43.

Theater der Jugend
With three stages, varied programmes from custard-pie comedy to rock'n'roll-style musical productions are offered.
Neubaugasse 38. Tel: 93 25 46.

MUSIC FOR YOUNG PEOPLE

The **Stadthalle** is the venue for major pop concerts and also stages sports events, spectaculars on ice and a horse show in November with a special afternoon session for children. In winter there is a circus.

Vogelweidplatz 14. Tel: 98 100.

The **Rockhaus** has a continuous programme of rock'n'roll, blues and reggae.

Adalbert-Stifter-Strasse 73. Tel: 33 46 41.

Some children may also enjoy the Vienna Boys Choir (see page 153 for details of performances).

MUSEUMS OF INTEREST TO CHILDREN

The Circus and Clown Museum

Karmelitengasse 9. Tel: 211 06-229. Open: Wednesday 5.30pm–7pm, Saturday 2.30pm–5pm, Sunday 10am–12 noon. Admission charge.

Museum of Natural History

Films in English are often shown on Sunday mornings.

Burgring 7 Maria-Theresien-Platz. Tel: 93 45 41. Open: Wednesday to Monday 9am–6pm. Admission charge.

Doll and Toy Museum

Schulhof 4 1st Floor. Tel: 535 68 60. Open: Tuesday to Sunday 10am–6pm. Admission charge.

Technisches Museum (Museum of Technology)

Mariahilfer Strasse 212. Tel: 89 101. Open: daily 9am–6pm, but closing temporarily for renovation in late 1992.

THE PRATER

The obvious place for a day out with the children is the Prater, offering not only a huge park in which to ramble, but also one of Europe's most celebrated fun-fairs. Highlights of the latter include the giant Ferris Wheel (details on pages 98–9), as well as the charming Lilliput train that winds through the meadow; there are the usual dodgems, roundabouts, ghost trains, slot machines and shooting ranges. Near by is the Planetarium (children's show on Sundays at 9.30am, closed August).

The **Spanish Riding School** appeals to all ages (see pages 70–1) and the zoo at Schönbrunn (open summer 9am–6pm, winter to 4pm) is worth a visit. More appealing is the game park of the **Lainzer Tiergarten** (Hermesstrasse, 13th District, open Easter to November, Wednesday to Sunday 8am–dusk). It contains deer, wild boar, horses, aurochs and moufflon.

The Circus and Clown Museum

CHRISTMAS IN VIENNA

The Christkindlmarkt in front of the City Hall lasts from about 16 November to Christmas. There are all sorts of trinkets to buy, seasonal gastronomic specialities, *Glühwein*, conjurors and much more. Open: 9am–8pm.

A smaller scale Christkindlmarkt takes place on Freyung (9am–7pm), with Christmas music daily at 6pm.

Sport

*T*he Viennese have skilfully exploited the natural potential of their surroundings for leisure and sport – for swimming and watersports on the Danube, for rambling or hiking in the Wienerwald and cycling round the city. With the exception of skiing and football, sports play a less important role in Austria than they do in Anglo-American culture, but tennis is beginning to break this pattern, partly due to the impact of tennis stars in neighbouring Germany.

AEROBICS/FITNESS CLUBS

There are many to choose from listed in the phone-book, two well-known ones are:

Club Danube *(Laxenburger Strasse 66, tel: 603 35 80)* which has four other branches and also offers tennis, squash and badminton and **Fit and Fun** *(Landstrasser Hauptstrasse 2a, tel: 72 66 89)*. Most have work-out machines and saunas. Some are for women only or for body-building.

BICYCLING

There are 250km of cycling routes in Vienna. Marked carriages on the underground or Schnellbahn (free on Sundays and holidays) show where bikes may be taken aboard (but not during rush hours). A half-price ticket is required. Good cycling areas are the Prater and the Danube Island.

Bicycle hire at **Vienna-Bike**, *(Salztorbrücke 1, Rechtes Donauufer, tel: 31 12 58)* and other locations, particularly around the Prater (see phone book under *Radverleih*).

BOATING/SAILING/ WINDSURFING

Boats can be hired locally on the Old Danube (Alte Donau). At the Freizeitzentrum on the New Danube wind-surfers are for hire.

Information about sailing from the **Austrian Yacht Club** *(Prinz-Eugen-Strasse 12, tel: 505 37 42)*.

On the Neusiedler See, near the Hungarian border (see page 139) there are ideal conditions for windsurfers.

BOWLING

Halls are located at **Prater Hauptallee** *124 (tel: 34 64 61)* and the **Bowlinghalle am Postsportplatz** *(Schumanngasse 107, tel: 46 43 61)*.

FOOTBALL

Matches are held in the Praterstadion, the Weststadion and elsewhere.

GOLF

Golf Connection *(Anton-Freunschlag-Gasse 34–52)* has an outdoor course *(Golf-Wien-Süd, tel: 69 41 87)* and an indoors club *(tel: 55 61 11)*, which includes practice tees, pitching and putting, instruction videos and a bar.

The **Vienna Golf Club** in the Prater *(Freudenaustrasse 65a, tel: 74 17 86)* has 18 holes and is technically a private club, but it may be possible to play.

Information also from the **Österreichischer Golfverband**, Haus des Sports, *(Prinz-Eugen-Strasse 12, tel: 505 37 42)*.

HIKING

The Presse- und Informationsdienst (Information Service) of the Rathaus (City Hall) issues leaflets with suggested hiking routes in the Wienerwald *(tel: 40-005)*. It is advisable to be inoculated against the ticks *(Zecken)* which are prevalent hereabouts and can cause meningitis, (pharmacists can supply the relevant information).

HORSE RACING

Flat-racing and steeplechasing in the season take place in the Freudenau (Prater) at Rennbahnstrasse 65. Trotting races are held all year round not far away in the **Krieau**. (Information from Haus des Sports, *Prinz-Eugen-Strasse 12, tel: 505 37 42.*)

HORSE RIDING
Wiener Reitinstitut,
(Barmherzigengasse 17, tel: 713 16 52) is a riding school and you can also ride in the Prater.

ICE-SKATING
Wiener Stadthalle
Vogelweidplatz 14. Tel: 98 100.
Eislaufverein
Lothringerstrasse 22. Tel: 713 63 53.

SQUASH

The phone-book lists a number of clubs, few of them, however, are near the centre.
Squash Club Top Fit
Erlachplatz 2-4. Tel: 62 24 45.

SWIMMING

Open-air baths (May to September) include the fashionable **Hietzinger Bad** *(Atzgersdorfer Strasse 14)*, the **Neuwaldegger Bad** *(Promenadegasse 58)* and the **Theresienbad**

A fine summer's day at the races

(Hufelandgasse 3).

Indoor baths include the **Amalienbad** *(Reumannplatz 9)*, the **Dianabad** *(Lilienbrunnengasse 7–9)* and the **Stadthalle** *(Vogelweidplatz 14)*.

Thermal baths at **Oberlaa** (Kurbadstrasse 14) and **Baden bei Wien**.

Nude bathing on the New Danube at Lobau.

TENNIS
Wien Sport
Bacherplatz. Tel: 54 31 310.
Tenniscenter La Ville
Kirchfeldgasse 3–5. Tel: 804 67 37.

There are many others, most with winter halls and floodlit courts.

SKIING

The nearest resort is the **Annaberg** near the shrine of Mariazell in the foothills of the Alps southwest of Vienna.

Viennese Cuisine

Viennese cuisine, like the city's inhabitants, is the product of diverse national influences and draws its inspiration from all the countries of the former Austro-Hungarian Empire. The *Knödel* (dumplings) are inherited from Bohemia, *Gulasch* and *Fogosch* (pike-perch) from Hungary, stuffed and red cabbage from the Slav lands further east. The *Wiener Schnitzel* has its counterpart in *piccata alla Milanese*, familiar to all who have travelled in north Italy. Only *Tafelspitz*, the tender boiled beef that was the Emperor Francis Joseph's favourite dish, appears to have an impeccable Viennese provenance.

Until the 1970s the city's chefs appeared to believe that quantity would make up for whatever was lacking in quality. The arrival of the Tyrolean Werner Matt at the Hilton changed all that. His 'nouvelle cuisine' approach caught on, and today many of the best establishments offer a sort of 'nouvelle Viennese cuisine'. To a new health-conscious generation this is a relief, although many a true Viennese still sticks to his cholesterol-laden diet, washed down with dry white wine or several *Krügerl* ($1/2$ litres) of beer. The visitor to Vienna can choose between a huge range of places to eat, while still eating 'Viennese': they include noisy *Beisln*, laid-back coffee-houses, bucolic *Heurigen* (wine-taverns), and, of course, the more pretentious restaurants offering specialities like *Tafelspitz*. In Vienna, both the gourmand and the gourmet will feel equally at home.

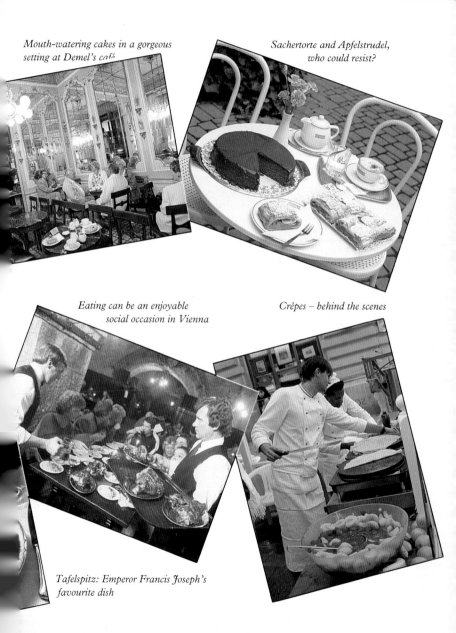

Mouth-watering cakes in a gorgeous setting at Demel's café

Sachertorte and Apfelstrudel, who could resist?

Eating can be an enjoyable social occasion in Vienna

Crêpes – behind the scenes

Tafelspitz: Emperor Francis Joseph's favourite dish

Restaurants and Beisln serving Viennese Cuisine

*A*s restaurant prices in other European countries (notably Italy) have become increasingly expensive, those in Vienna have been reasonably stable with the result that average establishments now look quite good value. VAT is levied on the food at 10 per cent and on the wine at 20 per cent.

A tip of 10 to 12$\frac{1}{2}$ per cent is expected and you will find that in most *Beisln* and coffee houses the waiter will add up the bill at your table and announce the result while proffering an account with various scrawled entries on it. Note, however, that bread is charged extra per piece. Aperitifs and liqueurs will inflate the bill spectacularly, as will a foreign bottle of wine.

Typical dishes and specialities

Backhendl chicken fried in breadcrumbs

Bauernschmaus mixed meat dish including roast pork, sausage, and smoked cuts served with dumplings and sauerkraut

Beuschel offal (heart and lung) in a spiced sauce

Blaukraut red cabbage

Blunzn black pudding

Buchteln or **Wuchteln** yeast dumplings with jam filling or vanilla sauce

Debreziner fatty sausage spiced with paprika

Eierschwammerln mushrooms (fresh mushroom soup – **Schwammerlsuppe** – is a speciality)

(Fleisch-)Laberln meat rissoles

Fisolen green beans

Fritattensuppe clear soup with crêpes

Germknödel yeast dumplings

Grießnockerlsuppe semolina dumpling soup

Guglhupf pound cake

Hischragout venison stew

Jägersalat salad of Chinese cabbage

Jungfernbraten loin of pork

Kaiserschmarrn omelette with raisins and plum compote

Kalbsvögerl knuckle of veal

Karree shoulder of pork (often smoked)

Knödel dumplings made from flour, potatoes, yeast etc

Krautfleckerl square pasta with seasonal cabbage

Krenfleisch boiled pork with grated horseradish

Leberknödel liver dumplings

Lungenbraten loin of pork

Millirahmstrudel (Milchrahmstrudel) strudel with a sweet cheese filling and vanilla sauce

Mohr im Hemd steamed pudding with nuts and chocolate

Nockerl home-made pasta

Palatschinken pancakes

Powidl thick plum jam

Rehfilet fillet of venison

Risipisi rice with peas, often served with **Kalbsvögerl**

Rollgerstlsuppe pearl barley soup

Rostbraten roast or a pan-fried sirloin steak

Schinkenfleckerln ham with square noodles
Semmelknödel bread dumplings seasoned with parsley and onion
Serviettenknödel similar to **Semmelknödel**
Stelze leg of veal or pork, roast or smoked
Tafelspitz tender boiled beef served with various sauces.
Topfenstrudel strudel from quark and sultanas
Vanillerostbraten garlic-seasoned beef
Vorspeise an entrée of hard-boiled eggs with a variety of sauces, cold meats, paté, etc
Wiener Schnitzel fillet of veal dipped in egg and breadcrumbs and fried golden brown. Many restaurants now only serve the version made with fillet of pork, not as good but cheaper.
Zwiebelrostbraten beef with crispy fried onions

Restaurants with good Viennese cooking

It is not necessary to go to a luxury restaurant to experience excellent Viennese cuisine. From a snack bar to a local *Beisl* Austrians enjoy good food. Although the fare can be a little heavy for some tastes, you will be unlikely to be disappointed with the dishes on offer. They will combine the best of the cuisines associated with Austria's past.

The following are all reasonably priced by Viennese standards, although eating the most expensive à la carte dishes and drinking bottled or foreign wine could push up the bill considerably in some cases. It is generally wise to reserve in advance.

Price ranges: (per head, without wine) **S** = 100–200 Austrian Schillings. **SS** 200–300. **SSS** 300–400. **SSSS** over 400 Schillings. It is sensible to enquire when booking which credit cards are accepted, if any.

S Figlmüller

A Viennese institution famous for the largest (pork) Wiener Schnitzel in town. *Wollzeile 5. Tel: 512 61 77. Open: Monday to Friday 7.30am–11pm, Saturday 7.30am–3pm. Closed: August, public holidays.*

SSS Hedrich

Very good cooking for the price, with fish a speciality. The service is faultless. *Stubenring 2. Tel: 512 95 88. Open: Monday to Friday 9am–9pm. Hot meals from 11.30am.*

SSS Hietzinger Bräu

The place for *Tafelspitz* fetishists and for beef generally. *Auhofstrasse 1. Tel: 87 77 087. Open: Monday to Saturday 11.30am–3pm and 6pm–11pm, Sunday 1.30pm–3pm. Closed: mid-July to mid-August.*

SS Salzamt

Outside seating in summer and fashionable bar. Apart from Viennese cooking there are Mediterranean dishes and their own inventions. *Ruprechtsplatz 1. Tel: 533 53 32. Open: daily 6pm–1am.*

SS Zur Goldenen Glocke

Agreeable garden restaurant in summer . *Kettenbrückengasse 9. Tel: 587 57 67. Open: Monday to Saturday 11.30am– 2.30pm and 5.30pm–midnight.*

SS Zum Schwarzen Kameel

Elegant luncheon restaurant in Jugendstil dining room next to the self-service and delicatessen. Excellent wines. *Bognergasse 5. Tel: 63 81 25. Open: Monday to Friday 9am–7pm, Saturday – 9am-2pm.*

BEISLN

The *Beisl* (or *Beisel*) is a name of Jewish origin implying a cheap eating-place serving traditional Viennese fare, often with a rustic ambience. In recent years the *Beisl* scene has enjoyed a Renaissance, although one result of this is the mushrooming of pseudo-*Beisln* whose prices, food and décor depart from tradition. *Stehbeisln*, where you eat your food standing at the counter are also popular. The following are well-known and combine honest food with atmosphere.

S Oswald und Kalb
Top quality Viennese and Styrian cooking.
Bäckerstrasse 14. Tel: 512 13 71. Open: daily 6pm–2am.

SSS Peter's Beisl
A *Beisl* at lunch-time but in the evening 'nouvelle cuisine' (Viennese style) predominates.
Arnethgasse 98. Tel: 46 53 75. Open: Tuesday to Sunday 10am–2am, hot meals 11.30am–11.30pm.

S Pfudl
Good home-cooking and modestly priced wine.
Bäckerstrasse 22. Tel: 512 67 05. Open: Monday to Friday 9am–midnight, Saturday 9am–3pm.

SS Stadtbeisl
Conveniently in the centre. More formal 'Hunter's Annexe' at the rear.
Naglergasse 21. Tel: 533 35 07. Open: daily 11am–midnight.

SS Zum Laterndl
The décor and atmosphere are authentic and the food is good.
Landesgerichtstrasse 12. Tel: 43 43 58. Open: Monday to Friday 10am–midnight. Hot meals 11.30am–2pm and 6pm–11.30pm.

EASTERN EUROPEAN AND BALKAN RESTAURANTS

Hungarian

SS Csárdásfürstin
Schwarzenbergstrasse 2. Tel: 512 92 46. Open: Monday to Saturday 7pm–1am.
S Ilona Stüberl
Good value home-cooking.
Bräunerstrasse 2. Tel: 533 90 29. Open: Monday to Saturday noon–3pm, 7pm–11pm.
SS Ungar-Grill
Burggasse 97. Tel: 93 52 38. Open: Monday to Saturday 6pm–1am.

Polish

S Polonez
Stuffed cabbage, caviar, vodka..
Wolfgang-Schmälzl-Gasse 8. Tel: 218 63 77. Monday to Friday 11am–3pm, 6pm–11pm, Sunday 11am–10pm.
S Winzerhaus
Cellar restaurant, music, dancing.
Rotenturmstrasse 17. Tel: 63 95 82. Open: Wednesday to Monday 10am–2am.

Rumanian

SS Bukarest
Bräunerstrasse 7. Tel: 512 37 63. Open: Tuesday to Sunday 11.30am–2.30pm, 6pm–midnight.

Russian

SSS Feuervogel
Alserbachstrasse 21. Tel: 34 10 392. Open: Monday to Saturday 6.30pm–1am. Closed: mid-July to mid-August.
SS Puschkin
Lederergasse 17a. Tel: 48 68 74. Open: Thursday to Tuesday 6pm–midnight. Friday and Saturday till 1am.

Yugoslavian

SS Dubrovnik
Am Heumarkt 5. Tel: 713 27 55 or 713 71 02. Open: daily 11am–3pm, 5.30pm– 11.30pm.

Greek

S Achilleus
Köllnerhofgasse 3. Tel: 512 83 28. Open: daily 11am–3pm, 5pm–midnight. In July, August evenings only.
SS Der Grieche, Panos Tsatsaris
Barnabitengasse 5. Tel: 587 74 66. Open: daily 11.30am–2.30pm, 6pm–midnight.

Turkish

SSS Kervansaray
Mahlerstrasse 9. Tel: 512 88 43. Open: Monday to Saturday noon–3pm, 6pm–1am.

OTHER NATIONAL CUISINES

Chinese

Astonishingly there are nearly 200 Chinese restaurants in Vienna, though only a few are worthy of note. Two are considered to stand out.

SSS China-Garden-Sichuan
Arbeiterstrandbadgasse 122. Tel: 23 67 71 72.
SSS Imperial Garden
Stubenring 18. Tel: 51 24 911. Open: Monday to Saturday noon–2.30pm, 7pm–11.30pm.

French

SSS Bistrot La Carafe
Karlsplatz 2. Tel: 65 04 87. Open: Monday to Saturday 5pm–midnight.
SSS Salut
Wildpretmarkt 3. Tel: 533 13 22. Open: Monday to Saturday 11.30am–2.30pm,

6pm–12.30pm. Closed: public holidays.

Indian

SS Koh-I-Noor
Marc-Aurel-Strasse 8. Tel: 533 00 80. Open: daily 11.30am–2.30pm, 6pm–11.30pm.
SS Maharadscha
Gölsdorfgasse 1. Tel: 63 74 43. Open: daily 11.30am–2.30pm, 6pm–midnight.

Italian

SSS Firenze
(Ristorante im Hotel Royal)
Tuscan specialities.
Singerstrasse 3. Tel: 52 46 31. Open: daily 11.30am–3pm, 6pm–midnight.
SSS La Ninfea
Schwarzspanierstrasse 18. Tel: 42 62 96. Open: Tuesday to Saturday noon–2.30pm, 6pm–11.30pm.
SS La Tavernetta
Good for fish.
Burggasse 44. Tel: 93 47 47. Open: Tuesday to Saturday noon–2.30pm, 6pm–11pm. Closed: 10–31 July.

Japanese

SSSS Mitsukoshi
Maysedergasse 5. Tel: 51 22 707. Open: Monday to Saturday noon–2pm, 6pm–midnight.
SSS Tokio
Börsegasse 3. Tel: 535 03 92. Open: daily 11.45am–2pm, 6pm–11pm.

Vegetarian

SS Siddharta
Fleischmarkt 16. Tel: 513 11 97. Open: Monday to Saturday 11.30am–3pm, 6pm–11pm, Sunday and public holidays 11.30am–3pm.

BEST RESTAURANTS

If price is no object, it is now possible to eat very well indeed in Vienna. The following have a reputation to keep up and seem to be doing so.

SSSS Altwienerhof
Fine cooking with a French flavour and one of the best wine lists in Vienna. Gourmets are happy to make the expedition to the 15th district.
Herklotzgasse 6. Tel: 83 71 45. Open: Monday to Friday 11.30–3pm, 6.30pm–midnight, Saturday 6.30pm–midnight.

SSSS Korso bei der Oper
Actually the restaurant of the Hotel Bristol. Highly original culinary ideas brilliantly carried out.

Mahlerstrasse 2. Tel: 515 16-546. Open: Sunday to Friday noon–3pm, 7pm–1am, Saturday 7pm–1pm. Closed: three weeks in August.

SSSS Palais Schwarzenberg
Apart from the excellent food the setting in the old palace, with a view of the park, makes dining here a very special experience.
Schwarzenbergplatz 9, Tel: 78 45 15–600. Open: daily noon–2.30pm, 6pm–midnight.

SSSS Steirereck
Probably the best exponent of the 'new Viennese' cuisine.
Rasumofskygasse 2. Tel: 713 31 68. Open; Monday to Friday noon–3pm, 7pm–midnight. Closed: public holidays.

Enjoying coffee in elegant surroundings

SSSS Vier Jahreszeiten
Crustaceans a speciality, imaginative presentation and exceptional wine list. (The restaurant is in the Inter-Continental Hotel.)
Johannesgasse 28. Tel: 711 22-143. Open: daily noon–3pm, 7pm–midnight. In summer. Closed: for Saturday lunch and Sunday dinner. Lunch at fixed price available.

SSSS Zu den drei Husaren
One of the most elegant restaurants in Vienna, famous *inter alia* for its noble ambience and fabulous *hors d'oeuvres*. Viennese haute cuisine at its best – this (one can well believe) was how the nobles of the Austro-Hungarian monarchy were served.
Weihburggasse 4. Tel: 51 21 092. Open: daily 6pm–1am.

Good food, pleasant ambience, reasonable prices

Bei Max *(Landhausgasse 2, tel: 63 73 59, SS)* is centrally placed, has a pleasant atmosphere and good Carinthian cooking. Near by is a charming small restaurant in the gallery running between the Herrengasse and Freyung – **Im Ferstel** *(Freyung 2, tel: 535 42 24, SS)*. **Do & Co** is not so cheap, but won't fail to please *(Akademiestrasse 3, tel: 512 64 74, SSS)*. **Eckel** *(Sieveringer Strasse 46, tel: 32 32 18, closed: Sunday and Monday, SSS)* will also set you back a bit, but is worth it for those lobsters and fruits de mer. You can also get lobster at the **Hummerbar,** on the first floor of the Kervansaray. **Kupferdachl** *(Schottengasse 7, tel: 63 93 81, SS)* has a reputation for excellent cooking and good service. **Der Pfiff um die Ecke** *(Wilhelm-Exner-Gasse 23,*

A delicious cold buffet at Café Demel

tel: 34 10 342, SSS) again offers first-class 'new Viennese' cooking, and laid-back service – it's very small, but handy for the Volksoper. **Push-In** *(Drahtgasse 3, off Judenplatz, tel: 53 53 945, SS)* is even more laid back, with a long oval bar-counter and just four tables – the drinks list is 16 times as long as the menu. **Schnattl** *(Lange Gasse 40, tel: 42 34 00, SS)* is where the media crowd like to hang out. A vegetarian restaurant with a good bar and wine list and excellent salads is **Wrenkh** *(Bauernmarkt 10, tel: 53 31 526, SS)*. **Dornbacher Strasse 123** is pretty far out *(at the end-stop of Tram 43)* but well worth an evening's excursion to **Gasthaus zum Herkner** *(tel: 45 43 86, SS)*. Herr Herkner boasts that he provides 'good homely cooking', but lucky the person who would have such a home and such cooking. This is a place where the celebrities come to tuck in, not to be seen.

'Zum Wohl!'
– what an Austrian Drinks

At the heart of the Austrian wine culture lies a contradiction: the locals are knowledgeable about their viticulture, yet content to drink vast quantities of indifferent, sometimes downright unpalatable, young white wine; in the *Heurigen* and cafés they often add mineral water to it *(Gespritzer)*. This is all the more remarkable because the best Austrian wine is very good indeed and keenly priced compared to French or even Italian wine.

The finest wines come from lower Austria (the *Weinviertel* and the *Wachau* in the Danube valley) and from Burgenland. Some good wine is also produced in Styria and on the outskirts of Vienna (Gumpoldskirchen is famous for its mellow white wines). The classic Austrian grape is the *Grüner Veltliner,* which produces an acidic white wine, extremely refreshing in the summer heat. Fruitier is the *Welschriesling* (Italian Riesling), and most noble is the *Rheinriesling* of the Wachau. The best red varieties are *Blaufränkisch*, dry and flavoursome, *Zweigelt* (dry with noticeable body) and *St Laurent* (sometimes really

excellent – smooth, fruity and elegant).

The beer-drinker in Austria is not so well-served as in Germany. The ubiquitous 50cl bottles of white (wheat) beer and dark ale from the big breweries like Schwechat and Ottakringer dominate the market, but their flavour is an acquired taste. The really appealing beer is available on draught *(vom Fass)*. Apart from popular draught brews like Schwechat 'Gold Fassl' and Zipfer 'Märzen', there are others well worth trying, such as Gösser, Hubertus Bräu and Puntigamer.

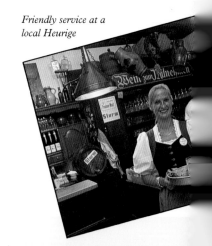

Friendly service at a local Heurige

Delicious wine on tap

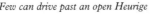

Few can drive past an open Heurige

Wine Cellars

*T*he tradition of wine cellars – both for storing wine and enjoying it – goes back to the early Middle Ages. Then, a contemporary visitor could claim that there was as much of Vienna below ground as above it; later, when the huge bell of St Stephen's was to be brought to the cathedral, a careful route had to be chosen so that the weight of it did not bring it crashing through the streets into the cellars below them. Both wine and food are modestly priced in *Weinkeller* locales (S–SS).

Figlmüller's Wiener Schnitzel

Esterházykeller *(Haarhof 1)*
The great noble family from Hungary kept wine from their estates here and gave the population the free run of it during the Turkish siege of 1683.

Melker Stiftskeller *(Schottengasse 3)*
Atmospheric vaulted chambers. Wine from the estates of the monastery of Melk.

Zwölf-Apostel-Keller *(Sonnenfels-gasse 3)*

There are baroque and medieval layers of this deep-sunken cellar. Cheap and rather boisterous, owing to the predominantly student clientèle.

Urbanikeller *(Am Hof)*
In a baroque patrician house.

Vis à Vis *(Wollzeile 5, opposite Figlmüller)*
A vast selection of fine wines by the glass.

Schnapps specialities also available. A good place to start getting to know the Austrian wine varieties.

Wein Comptoir *(Bäckerstrasse 6)*
An up-market selection of wines and food
– reservations required (tel: 512 17 60).

Weinmuseum *(Weihburggasse 20)*
A wine-bar rather than a cellar. Some
100 open wines on offer with appropriate
light snacks, cheeses, etc. You can buy
bottles to take away at shop prices.

BEER STÜBERLN

Bierhof *(Naglergasse 13)*
Large selection of beers and some
interesting mixed drinks involving beer.

Gösser Bräu Smutny *(Elisabeth-
strasse 3)*
Solid Viennese cooking and good beer
from the barrel.

Krah-Krah *(Rabensteig 8)*
The largest selection of beers in town,
bottled or on draught.

HEURIGEN S–SS

The Heurigen villages (see pages 126–7)
lie like a necklace around the periphery
of Vienna to the south, southwest and
northwest. Many *Heurigen* offer hot
dishes such as roast pork and fried
chicken, the fat and crackling of the pork
being a good counterpoint to the tart
young white wines, which in turn provide
plenty of gastric acid to mop up the rich
fat. However, many people prefer to
accompany their drinking with a heaped
plate of mixed salad, an assortment of
cheeses and hunks of fresh bread.

There is such a vast number of
establishments to choose from that any
selection is bound to be rather arbitrary.
The following are unlikely to disappoint.
Those mentioned all have gardens
(usually looking on to the owners' own
vineyards). Opening seasons of *Heurigen*
are not always fixed, but are generally
between March and October (or as long

as the new wine lasts in the case of
genuine *Heurigen*). The daily press may
be consulted to see which are open or the
signposts in the villages themselves.
Generally, *Heurigen* are open from mid-
afternoon to late in the evenings; at
weekends also for lunch.

Renowned Heurigen entertainment

Altes Presshaus
Grinzing – Cobenzlgasse 15. Tel: 32 23 93.

Fuhrgassl-Huber
Neustift am Walde 68. Tel: 44 14 05.

Mayer am Platz
*Beethovenhaus, Pfarrplatz 2, Heiligenstadt.
Tel: 37 12 87.*

Zimmermann
*Armbrustergasse 5, Heiligenstadt. Tel: 37
22 11.*

For modest traditional *Heurigen*, usually
family-run, it is worth exploring the
villages of Mauer, Salmannsdorf and
Stammersdorf.

Cafés

*T*he Viennese café (see pages 54-5) is a place to meet your friends, write postcards, read the newspaper or simply gaze into space. Most offer a variety of hot dishes and an even greater variety of coffee.

COFFEE CULTURE

The legend says that coffee beans were left behind by the Turks after the siege of 1683. A shrewd entrepreneur, having discovered that they were not food for the camels as previously thought, is supposed to have opened the first coffee-house named the Blue Bottle. In fact, there is evidence that coffee had been known in Vienna since 1645. Probably the first coffee-house was opened by an Armenian, Johannes Diodato, in 1685.

The Viennese are very fussy about their coffee. Here are just some of the commoner forms.

Einspänner espresso in a glass with whipped cream
Eiskaffee vanilla ice in a glass, cold espresso and whipped cream
Grosser or **kleiner Schwarzer** or **Brauner** large or small black or white coffee
Kapuziner cappuccino
Kurzer strong black espresso
Maria Theresia espresso laced with orange liqueur, cream and sugar
Melange coffee with milk and (usually) a cream froth
Mocca g'spritzt espresso laced with rum or cognac
Obermeier espresso to which cream is added by pouring it over the curved side of a spoon
Schale Gold espresso with cream served in a tea-cup

Atmospheric cafés:

Bräunerhof *(Stallburggasse 2)*
Music at weekends. Sometimes literary events.

Central *(Herrengasse 14/Strauchgasse)*
In the elegant setting of Ferstel Palais. Not the cheapest.

Diglas *(Wollzeile 10)*
Good food, draught beer.

Dommayer *(Dommayergasse 1 – Hietzing)*
Where Lanner and Strauss once played.

Griensteidl *(Michaelerplatz)*
Newly opened. Good food.

Hawelka *(Dorotheergasse 6)*
Legendary Bohemian café

Landtmann *(Dr-Karl-Lueger-Ring 4)*
Very political.

Ministerium *(Georg-Coch-Platz 4)*
The officials from the nearby ministries know value for money and come here.

Museum *(Friedrichstrasse 6)*
Originally dubbed 'Café Nihilismus', as designed by Adolf Loos.

Prückel *(Stubenring 24)*
Very traditional with card tables, etc.

Schwarzenberg *(Kärntner Ring 17)*
Oldest Ringstrasse café.

Sperl *(Gumpendorfer Strasse 11)*
Traditional, billiards, etc.

Tirolerhof *(Führichgasse 8)*
Best *Apfelstrudel* in town.

KONDITOREIEN (patisseries)

The distinction between a café and a Konditorei may seem a fine one to the outsider, but in Vienna no one would confuse the two. The main function of the Konditorei is to provide the ultimate baroque experience of sugared pastries, fruit slices topped with meringue and an array of cakes not dreamed of in the kitchens of more prosaic lands. Many of these, like other items of Viennese cuisine, have their origins in the lands of the former Austro-Hungarian Monarchy (for example the Dobosch, Esterházy and Malakoff cakes). Some people may find a lot of these offerings too sweet, in which case the ones to go for are those with Joghurt (yoghurt) in the ingredients, or those featuring jellied soft fruits: *Erdbeeren* (strawberries), *Himbeeren* (raspberries), *Preiselbeeren* (cranberries) or *Heidelbeeren* (bilberries).

Demel *(Kohlmarkt 14)*

Why do people still flock to Demel although the prices are high, the seating spectacularly uncomfortable and the acoustics so bad that you get the second or third ricochet of your fellow guests' conversation more clearly than your own words? The reason is that Demel is an institution, gastronomically speaking the most distinguished relic of Imperial and Royal Vienna. There is an alluring buffet near the entrance which also offers *Leckerbissen* (delicacies) to tempt you to light lunch. They make their own pastries, cakes and praline chocolates. The décor and the mirror room are an experience themselves.

Gerstner *(Kärntner Strasse 11–15)*

Coffee and ice-cream specialities. The window seats look on to the fashionable shopping mall below.

Heiner *(Kärntner Strasse 21–23 and Wollzeile 9)*

Another 'Imperial and Royal' confectioner. The branch in the Wollzeile with a Biedermeier interior is particularly attractive. Diabetic recipes on offer.

Kurcafé-Konditorei Oberlaa *(Neuer Markt 16)*

A newcomer which has been so successful that they have been able to open three branches.

Lehmann *(Graben 12)*

Some tasty light lunch dishes as well as good pastries here.

Sluka *(Rathausplatz 8)*

Good buffet and cakes, elegant atmosphere. Not one of the cheapest places.

Delicious Viennese pastries

Cheap Eating

*E*ating cheaply in Vienna is partly an art and partly a science. The art consists in choosing carefully in an establishment that has a large menu with some cheap dishes, and always confining yourself to the house wine or a beer. Many of the places already mentioned (*Heurigen*, Kellers, Cafés and *Beisln*) can qualify as reasonably cheap if this approach is adopted, with some main courses that are adequate for a whole meal (especially at lunch-time) costing 70-80 Schillings. The science consists in knowing which places are actually in business to be cheap, but which nevertheless provide something edible or even tasty.

Typical butcher's shop

Würstelstände – S

All over the city, usually on or near traffic connections, are the celebrated *Würstelstände* or sausage bars. Their fat-filled offerings may not constitute a very healthy diet, but they certainly fill you up. The staple item is a *Burenwurst,* greasy and spicy, apparently deriving its name from a Boer recipe imported from north Germany. Eat this and you will understand why Boer cuisine has not conquered the world. *Frankfurters* and *Debreziners* are also available, to be eaten with hot gherkins, sauerkraut and a dash of mustard, and possibly a Kaiser–semmel roll. The alarmingly named *Teufelsroller* (rollmops) are no doubt healthier, but the sweating *Leberkäse* (meat-loaf) is not.

Butchers' Shops, Grocers – S

A speciality of Vienna are the butchers' shops with a small *Stehbeisl* (self-service with a stand-up counter) attached. The meat and offal are guaranteed fresh and beer is on offer. Try the *Ziegler* in the Krugerstrasse, just off the Kärntner Strasse. For luxury snacks try the *Julius Meinl* grocers (corner of Graben and Naglergasse, and on the Opernring). The basement of the *Herzmansky* store (Mariahilfer Strasse 26–30) has a selection of up-market small eateries serving fish, crêpes, meat snacks, etc.

Crêperie, Kärntner Strasse

Self-service chains – S

In recent years a great boon has been visited upon Vienna, namely the *Naschmarkt* self-service restaurants, so christened after the city's famous open-air market on the Wienzeile. They exist at Schottengasse 1, Mariahilfer Strasse 85 and Schwarzenbergplatz. There is a degree of individuality, at least in the hot dishes on offer from the different branches. Perhaps the best is the one on Schwarzenbergplatz, with a large seating area pleasantly decorated in late art nouveau style. The food ranges from open sandwiches to grills and fish dishes and a good selection of desserts. Wine from the barrel, draught beer and espresso coffee complete the menu.

All grills are cooked while you wait and are of the highest quality. There is something to suit virtually every taste and every pocket.

Nordsee – S

The *Nordsee* chain of fish restaurants allow rather less variation from their standard fare (plaice and chips, halibut, paella, etc), but it is always satisfying: Kohlmarkt 6, Naschmarkt, Kärntner Strasse 25, Mariahilfer Strasse 34 and 84, Neubaugasse 9, and elsewhere.

Wienerwald – S

A long-established chain with solid, reliable food and very moderate prices. Not self-service. Freyung 6 (Schottenkeller), Bellariastrasse 12, Mariahilfer Strasse 156, Argentinierstrasse 66 and elsewhere (more towards the suburbs than in the centre).

Sandwich Bars – S

The Viennese sandwich bars are by no means culinary black holes. The best of them serve mouth-watering open sandwiches consisting of combinations of *Aufstriche*, or purées of fish, meat, vegetables and scrambled egg. There are several around the centre, but one in particular stands out: **Trzesniewski**, Dorotheergasse 1.

Mouth-watering display of bread

G'moa-Keller (Am Heumarkt 25) **– S**
Run by the formidable Novak sisters, this is one of the most idiosyncratic locales in Vienna. The chopped liver is excellent, the open wine good. It is possible you will not be let in if they don't like the look of you, as Frau Novak is fond of observing, 'I threw the chancellor out once...'.

Hotel Tips

*T*he choice of accommodation in Vienna ranges from baroque palaces doing service as luxury hotels to modest family-run guest houses and youth hostels. The Vienna Tourist Board supplies a listing of all establishments categorised by them according to a star-rating system – five stars for a luxury hotel, four stars for first class accommodation, three stars for middle class, two for simple and one for modest. Apart from the hotels there are pensions (also graded) and seasonal hotels, the latter being students' hostels turned into hotels during the summer months. The leaflet indicates the number of rooms and suites, prices with or without bath/shower, and those which are 'cyclophile' for cyclists. It also shows which establishments are family run.

Tourist Information Centres provide general hotel information and those at the main railway stations and the airport will help you book a room. Booking facilities also at the offices at Kärntner Strasse 38, and at the Accommodation Bureau in the Opern Passage.

In the high season, which lasts from April to October, prices will be higher and rooms often hard to come by – it is advisable to book through your travel agent in advance.

Service charges are added to bills, but the customary tips for porters,

waiters, etc are expected. Always ask the concierge about the rate charged for phone calls from your room. Some travellers have had a nasty shock when discovering items on the bill representing phone calls charged at up to 200 per cent of the cost! Another area of dispute can be calls booked to you but not made by you, so it is wise to keep a note of the time and duration of calls made.

It is also better to change money in banks at the official rate – many (but not all) hotels give a very poor rate. Complaints about hotels can be directed to the Vienna Tourist Board, A-1025 Vienna, Obere Augartenstrasse 40.

Hotel Sacher: home of the original Viennese Sachertorte

PRICES

Price ranges for the five categories of hotels are as follows (assuming room with bath; prices in Austrian Schillings).

	Single	Double *(per person)*
5–star	2,000–4,000	1,500–2,700
4–star	1,200–1,500	700–1,300
3–star	600–1,000	450–750
2–star	400–750	300–500
1–star	300–500	250–450

Seasonal hotels, open 1 July to 30 September (single) 300–500 (double) 250–400.

The most expensive (4–star) pensions will cost around 700–900 for a single, 500–700 per person for a double. The cheapest (1–star) will cost around 300–400 for a single, 250–350 per person for a double.

A number of hotels and pensions offer a special deal between 7 November and 30 March for weekends, whereby you can stay for three nights and pay only for two. Details from the Winter Leaflet of the Vienna Tourist Board or travel agents.

Vienna's Hotel Imperial

LOCATION

Vienna is extremely compact, as far as the main places of interest to tourists are concerned: the 'old city' was hermetically sealed until the demolition of the fortifications in 1857, meaning that the bulk of the buildings dating from baroque times or earlier are within a corset or are on the edge of it, but there is also plenty of accommodation in every other price category to be found here. Pensions can be most central of all – there is a small one on the Graben itself – although those in more favoured positions are naturally not so cheap.

The advantages of being in the old city, especially for elderly visitors, scarcely need underlining: short walks to see specific sites are always possible. In the vast majority of cases you have only a short and pleasant walk back to your hotel afterwards. The streets are well lit and safe, and there are substantial areas closed to cars altogether. The only possible problem could be noise, but this is only likely to be a nuisance in cheaper establishments with inferior insulation, and even then only in the rooms looking on to the street. The luxury hotels, of course, have double glazing and air conditioning.

Hotels

The recently opened Vienna Marriott

Jahreszeiten). The **SAS Palace** is much favoured by businessmen and one reason may be its restaurant, which is famous for its steaks (**Le Siècle im Ersten**).

Traditional Viennese or International Sophistication?
The choice here will presumably be dictated by whether your visit is for pleasure or business. Obviously the recently opened Vienna Marriott has everything the businessman could want from conference rooms to a gym, and the other local branches of big inter-national chains are to a greater or lesser extent similarly equipped. However, to savour the charm of something more specifically Viennese in taste or décor, you could turn to a hotel like the **König von Ungarn** (itself a converted baroque building) or the **Palais Schwarzenberg**, where the walls of the bedrooms are

Baroque Hotel König von Ungarn

Hotels with haute cuisine
A feature of Vienna that is more pronounced than in most European capitals is that the cuisine in the best hotels aspires to the highest gourmet standards (that is, they do not just serve 'international' food). It is not quite true to say that the five best hotels have the five best restaurants in the city, but they are certainly among the best. In these cases the restaurant is under the command of a (usually well-known) chef, who has total discretion in preparing the menus, and in many cases creates his own dishes. Hotels with this type of cuisine include the **Bristol** (the Korso restaurant), the **Hilton** (the Prinz Eugen), the **Imperial** (Zur Majestät) and the **Inter-Continental** (the Vier

Hotel Sacher has international appeal

adorned with 19th-century Viennese history paintings. And, of course, **Sacher**, the most celebrated traditional hotel in Vienna, with its elegant sitting rooms, retains the aura of a bygone and more leisured age. But you need not go to such heights of luxury to savour family-style Viennese hospitality: the previously mentioned *Hotels and Pensions List* of the Vienna Tourist Board has a special sign for family-run establishments.

Pensions
Unlike many Italian pensions, Viennese ones (with a very few exceptions) confine themselves to bed and breakfast. The better ones are still not exactly cheap, but they provide something different from the impersonality of a hotel. Many have their *Stammgäste* (regulars), who

may be visiting scholars or Austrians from the provinces, and the number of rooms they have is often very limited. For this reason it is best to make arrangements well in advance and ensure that you have written confirmation of your booking. Pensions are obviously ideal for people staying a little longer than average, who are perhaps doing research or such like, and who welcome the peace and quiet and family atmosphere of such places.

Seasonal Hotels
For those who want something really informal, the generally cheap Seasonal Hotels (3–star to 1–star categories) provide friendly no-frills service – often the college students themselves are doing the catering. In the summer months these may be the best bet for the bike tourer – those that cater for cyclists are listed in the Tourist Board brochure.

Practical Guide

ARRIVING

British and North American passport-holders do not require visas for Austria for visits of up to three months' duration. There are no obligatory inoculations.

Vienna's Schwechat International Airport is 19km east of the city, about 20 minutes by bus (tickets from the driver). There are two buses, one to the City Air Terminal at the Vienna Hilton Hotel, and one to the Westbahnhof, calling on the way at the Südbahnhof. They run to the City Terminal every half-hour from 6am to 8am, and every 20 minutes from 8am to 7.20pm. Thereafter at longer intervals. To the Südbahnhof/ West-bahnhof the service runs every half-hour between 7am and 7pm.

A train service also runs from the airport every hour between 7.30am and 8.30pm stopping at Wien Mitte (City Air Terminal) and Wien Nord (Praterstern). The journey lasts 30 minutes and is the cheapest way to the centre.

Taxis are also available, and might cost up to 600 Schillings into town, depending on destination. The journey lasts 20 to 30 minutes.

AUSTRIAN AIRLINE SERVICES

UK: 50 Conduit Street, London WIR ONP (tel: (071) 439 0741)
US: Fifth Floor, 608 Fifth Avenue, New York, NY 10020 (tel: (212) 307 6227 or (212) 265 6350)

All other major or national carriers in Europe fly to Vienna.

BABYSITTERS

The **Babysitterzentrale** *(tel: 95 11 35)* has minders between the ages of 16 and 60 with foreign languages. Call them Monday to Friday 8am–3pm.

CAMPING

The nearest camping sites to the centre are:
Campingplatz Wien West I
(Hüttelbergstrasse 40, A–1140, tel: 94 14 49), April to October
Campingplatz Wien West II
(Hüttelbergstrasse 80, A–1140, tel: 94 23 14), open all year round
Campingplatz Wien Süd
(Breitenfurterstrasse 269, tel: 86 92 18), May to September

CARS

Breakdown

In the event of a breakdown there are two efficient motoring clubs with international affiliation: ÖAMTC, (Schubertring 1–3, tel: 71 19 90) and ARBÖ (Mariahilfer Strasse 80, tel: 85 35 35). They will also supply more general advice regarding insurance, route-planning and repairs. Although they will examine your vehicle and carry out emergency repairs to get you going, general repairs have to be done in a garage. They can direct you to one appropriate for your model.

Driving

Driving in Vienna is not easy for the uninitiated: one-way streets proliferate, tramways complicate and parking is difficult. In the Inner City and some parts of the suburbs there is a short-term parking system, indicated by a blue line and a street sign.

You need a book of dated tickets obtainable for a small fee from 'Tabak' shops; the ticket must be displayed, showing the time and date when you parked. The allowed period is 1½ hours. Spacious underground parking in the Inner City is available on the motorised part of the Kärntner Strasse (beside the Opera), on Stephansplatz, on Freyung and in front of the Rathaus (City Hall).

Third party insurance is obligatory and it is advisable to obtain a Green card from your insurance company. Seatbelts are compulsory. Children under the age of 12 years are not allowed in the front seats. Avoid using the horn except in dire emergencies.

Traffic regulations

These include priority for those coming from the right, except where the road you are on is indicated as the major road

No parking: bane of the motorist

(Vorrang). Particular care is required with trams, when turning across their tracks (the tram always has priority). The Ringstrasse is one-way for vehicles, but trams run both ways on opposite sides of it. Viennese drivers are inclined to be aggressive and impatient but allowance is usually made for a foreign number plate. The speed limit is 50km. Illegal parking often results in towing away.

Car Rental

Car rental is available from **Avis** (Opernring 1, tel: 58 76 241, or at Schwechat Airport, tel: 711 10-2700). **Budget** (Wien Hilton, tel: 75 65 65–0), **Europcar** (Parkring 12, tel: 51 55 30, or Schwechat Airport, tel: 711 10-0) and **Hertz** (Ungargasse 37, tel: 713 15 96–0, or Schwechat Airport, tel: 77 70 26 61). British citizens need only a valid driving licence; US and Australian citizens need to obtain an International Driving Licence before departure.

CHURCHES AND OTHER PLACES OF WORSHIP

Anglican
(Jaurésgasse 17–19, tel: 723 15 75)
Catholic
(English language, Boltzmanngasse 7, tel: 515 52 375)
Baptist
(Hochmaisgasse 8–10, tel: 804 92 59)
Jewish
(Seitenstettengasse 4, tel: 36 16 55)
Islamic
(Am Hubertusdamm 17-19, tel: 30 13 89-0)
Lutheran
(Dorotheergasse 18, tel: 512 83 92)
Methodist
(Sechshauser Strasse 56, tel: 83 62 67)
Reformed Church
(Evangelist, Dorotheergasse 16, tel: 512 83 93)

CLIMATE

Vienna's average yearly temperature is around 10°C, a statistic which rather masks the severe cold in the depths of winter, with sub-zero daytime temperatures not infrequent, and the extreme heat in mid-summer.

CONVERSION TABLE

FROM	TO	MULTIPLY BY
Inches	Centimetres	2.54
Centimetres	Inches	0.3937
Feet	Metres	0.3048
Metres	Feet	3.2810
Yards	Metres	0.9144
Metres	Yards	1.0940
Miles	Kilometres	1.6090
Kilometres	Miles	0.6214
Acres	Hectares	0.4047
Hectares	Acres	2.4710
Gallons	Litres	4.5460
Litres	Gallons	0.2

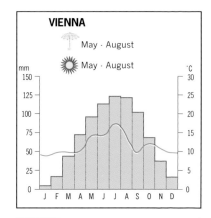

VIENNA

☂ May - August

☀ May - August

Weather Chart Conversion
25.4mm = 1 inch
$°F = 1.8 × °C + 32$

Ounces	Grams	28.35
Grams	Ounces	0.0353
Pounds	Grams	453.6
Grams	Pounds	0.0022
Pounds	Kilograms	0.4536
Kilograms	Pounds	2.205
Tons	Tonnes	1.0160
Tonnes	Tons	0.9842

Men's Suits

UK		36	38	40	42	44	46	48
Rest of Europe	46	48	50	52	54	56	58	
US		36	38	40	42	44	46	48

Dress Sizes

UK		8	10	12	14	16	18
France		36	38	40	42	44	46
Italy		38	40	42	44	46	48
Rest of Europe		34	36	38	40	42	44
US		6	8	10	12	14	16

Men's Shirts

UK	14	14.5	15	15.5	16	16.5	17
Rest of Europe	36	37	38	39/40	41	42	43
US	14	14.5	15	15.5	16	16.5	17

Men's Shoes

UK	7	7.5	8.5	9.5	10.5	11
Rest of Europe	41	42	43	44	45	46
US	8	8.5	9.5	10.5	11.5	12

Women's Shoes

UK	4.5	5	5.5	6	6.5	7
Rest of Europe	38	38	39	39	40	41
US	6	6.5	7	7.5	8	8.5

CRIME

Vienna is one of the safest capital cities in Europe. Subways are well-lit and police patrols in the city centre are well-coordinated. In the event of an emergency, the police can be called on 133.

CRISIS LINE

Befrienders, an organisation to render advice and assistance in a crisis, operates from *Seidlgasse 8, 1st Floor (tel: 713 33 74 – English spoken)*. The line is open daily 10am–1pm, 7pm–10pm; also late Friday night until 7am Saturday morning.

A new initiative of the Austrian Broadcasting Corporation (ORF) and the Ministry for Social Welfare is the so-called *Kummer Nummer* (Worry Number, **54 70 46**). The helpers operate in 13 languages and deal with specific problems involving professional bodies, the bureaucracy etc.

CUSTOMS REGULATIONS

Duty-free quotas for those aged 17 or over are: 200 cigarettes, 50 cigars, or 250g of tobacco; 1 litre of spirits or 2.25 litres of wine. Personal possessions are not dutiable, and neither are presents up to a value of 400 Austrian Schillings. You may bring in any amount of Austrian or foreign currency and export up to 15,000 Austrian Schillings or any amount of foreign currency.

DISABLED PEOPLE

Vienna is above average in its facilities for disabled people, and the newest underground stations on the U3 have lifts that can accommodate wheelchairs; main museums have ramps and many hotels have rooms for the handicapped. Advice is available from **Allgemeine Unfallversicherungsanstalt**, *Adalbert-Stifter-Strasse 65–7, tel: 331 11)*. There are general facilities for the disabled at Schwechat Airport. The **Bundesbahn** (Federal Railway) issues lightweight portable wheelchairs for use on trains. They are gratis but must be booked at least three days in advance at any railway station.

ELECTRICITY

220 volts, 50 cycle AC throughout Austria. Two-pin round plugs are standard.

EMBASSIES AND CONSULATES

Australia *Mattiellistrasse 2–4, tel: 512 85 80;* **Canada** *Dr-Karl-Lueger-Ring 10, tel: 533 36 91;* **Ireland** *Hilton Center, Landstrasser Haupt–strasse 2, tel: 715 42 46;* **New Zealand** *Lugeck 1, tel: 512 66 36;* **UK** *Jaurésgasse 12, tel: 75 61 17 (Consulate);* **USA** *Garten-baupromenade 2, tel: 31 55 11 (Consulate)*

EMERGENCY TELEPHONE NUMBERS

Ambulance	*(Rettung): 144*
Fire Brigade	*(Feuerwehr): 122*
Police	*(Polizei): 133*

Thomas Cook travellers' cheque loss or theft: 0660 6266 (local call rates). The branch listed on page 190 can give emergency assistance.

ENTERTAINMENT INFORMATION – PRIOR BOOKING

The most useful tool for the tourist is the monthly programme of events issued by the Vienna Tourist Board and available at all Tourist Information Offices. It is printed in three languages and covers, for each day of the month, all performances of opera, theatre and fringe theatre, together with concerts, exhibitions, lectures, walking tours and even balls in the season. Addresses with telephone numbers are printed under each venue. The only entertainment not covered in this is commercial films, for which the daily newspapers have to be consulted (films in English are indicated by the rubric OF following a title printed in English).

For prior booking for the Staatsoper, the Volksoper, the Burgtheater and the Akademietheater you may apply to the **Österreichischer Bundes-theaterverband** Bestellbüro (National Ticket Office) at *Hanuschgasse 3/ Goethegasse 1 (tel: 514 44/2690/2959 – credit cards 513 15 13, Monday to Friday 8am– 6pm, Saturday 9am–2pm, Sunday 9am–noon)*. In addition, each venue has its own advance ticket office, although for more informal events and fringe performances you will only be able to buy a ticket on the spot.

It is possible to buy tickets from agencies (**Theaterkartenbüros**) around the city centre or often through your hotel, but both of these methods involve very hefty commissions. Do not be misled by tickets (returns) advertised in agency windows with the seat price printed on them – you will still have to pay the commission on top (about 20 per cent).

Tickets for the main theatres are generally on sale one week before the performance, for musical events about one month. Remaining places are bought at the theatre's **Abendkassa**, which opens an hour before curtain up. Written bookings from abroad (or elsewhere in Austria) must arrive at least 14 days before the date required at the National Ticket Office. An agency specialising in supplying tickets against bookings from abroad is the Vienna *Ticket Service, Postfach 160, A-1060, tel: 587 98 43*. Write a month in advance.

HEALTH

A reciprocal agreement exists between the UK and Austria to provide British citizens with free emergency treatment following accidents or sudden illness (but full payment has to be made for medication). It is, however, sensible to take out private medical insurance for your trip – normal treatment must be paid for and is not cheap. Larger hotels have a doctor on call, and others can call the **Notarzt** *(emergency doctor, tel: 141)* if necessary. The system is extremely efficient. The majority of doctors speak at least some English. Your consulate can also supply a list of English-speaking doctors and dentists. Americans may find the **Medical Society of Vienna**, *(Lazarettgasse 13, tel: 42 45 68) helpful.*

HOLIDAYS

On public and religious holidays shops and places of work are closed with the exception of restaurants, newspaper stalls at railway stations and similar. The following are holidays: New Years Day, 6 January (Epiphany), Easter Monday, 1 May (Labour Day), Ascension Day, Whit Monday, Corpus Christi, 15 August (Assumption of Mary), 26 October (National Day), 1 November

(All Saints' Day), 8 December (Immaculate Conception), 25 December (Christmas Day) and 26 December (St Stephen's). Where no date is given the holidays are variable according to the calendar. Some other days are virtually holidays, in that many people take the day off – eg Good Friday, 2 November (All Souls), Christmas Eve and 31 December.

The Rathaus by night

LANGUAGE
Knowledge of English is widespread in Vienna, and a phrase-book should fill in the gaps of basic communication.

Days of the week
Montag Monday
Dienstag Tuesday
Mittwoch Wednesday
Donnerstag Thursday
Freitag Friday
Samstag Saturday
Sonntag Sunday

Months
Jänner January
Februar February
März March
April April
Mai May
Juni June
Juli July
August August

September September
Oktober October
November November
Dezember December

Numbers
eins one
zwei two
drei three
vier four
fünf five
sechs six
sieben seven
acht eight
neun nine
zehn ten

Words/Phrases
ja yes
nein no
bitte please
danke (schön) thank you (very much)
guten Morgen good morning
guten Abend good afternoon/evening
gute Nacht good night
klein small
gross large
schnell quickly
kalt cold
warm hot
gut good
Weisswein white wine
Rotwein red wine
Brot bread
Milch milk
Wasser water
rechts on the right
links on the left
offen open
geschlossen closed
nahe near
weit far
immer geradeaus straight ahead
wieviel how much?
teuer expensive
billig cheap

LIBRARY

The British Council (Schenkenstrasse 4, A-1010 Wien, tel: 533 26 16) has a large library and a selection of English newspapers and journals.

LOST PROPERTY

The Lost Property Office of the Viennese Police Headquarters (Fundamt) is at Wasagasse 22 (tel: 313 44– 9211). Articles left on trams and buses may turn up in the Lost Property of Vienna Transport (tel: 65 930– 0). The central railway Lost Property is at the Westbahnhof, Langauergasse 2.

MONEY

The currency unit is the Austrian Schilling, divided into 100 Groschen. Coins are in denominations of 5, 10 and 50 Groschen and 1, 5, 10 and 20 Schillings. Notes are 20, 50, 100, 500, 1,000 and 5,000 Schillings.

Wechselstuben (exchange bureaux) are open daily at Schwechat Airport (arrivals 8.30am– 11.30pm, departures 6am– 9pm), City Air Terminal (Monday to Saturday 9am–noon, 1pm– 6pm, Sunday 9am–1pm), Westbahnhof (7am– 10pm), and Südbahnhof (6.30am– 10pm). Banks are open Monday to Friday 8am-3pm (Thursdays until 5.30pm). Most branch offices close between 12.30pm and 1.30pm for lunch.

Credit cards and travellers' cheques are widely accepted, as are Eurocheques. Travel agents and hotels also change money. Thomas Cook travellers' cheques free you from the hazards of carrying cash. In the event of loss or theft, the Thomas Cook refund service is available 24 hours a day, every day (see page 183).

NEWSPAPERS

The leading English newspapers and the *Wall Street Journal* are on sale in Vienna.

OPENING TIMES

Museums: see individual entries.
Pharmacies: Monday to Friday 8am– noon and 2pm– 6pm, Saturdays 8am– 12 noon. In the window will be the address of the nearest 24–hour pharmacy (*Apotheke*). English-speaking pharmacists at Internationale Apotheke, Kärntner Ring 17. Tel: 512 28 25.
Post office: Monday to Friday 8am– 6pm. The central post office is open on Saturday 8am– noon (Barbaragasse 2) and post offices at Westbahnhof and Südbahnhof are open round the clock, also at weekends.
Shops: Monday to Friday 8am– 6.30pm, Saturdays 8am– 1pm. (See **Shopping** for extended hours.)

Catching up on the news of the day

Hopping on or off a tram

PUBLIC TRANSPORT

The Vienna public transport system is among the best in Europe. It comprises buses, metro (*U-Bahn*), trams (*Strassen–bahn*) and a rapid transit railway (*S-Bahn*), all systems dovetailing with each other extremely well. The central office of the *Wiener Verkehrsbetriebe* (Vienna Transport Authority) in the underpass at Karlsplatz supplies a map of the system, together with leaflets dealing with night-buses, regulations or taking bicycles on to public transport. (These are in German however.)

There are a number of possibilities for buying tickets for multiple journeys economically. You should avoid trying to buy a ticket from the machine on the tram itself – it requires quite a complicated combination of small change and costs more than a unit of a ticket purchased in advance.

All tickets must be validated in the machines placed near the doors of buses and trams or at the entrances to the metro stations. (The machine stamps a time and date on a blank unit of the ticket.)

The different types of tickets that can be purchased in advance from *Tabak/Trafik* (newsagent and tobacconist kiosks) or offices of the *Wiener Verkehrsbetriebe* are as follows: a block of five or 10 single journey tickets, (not very economic); a 24-hour season ticket (*24-Stunden-Netzkarte*) for unlimited journeys on all forms of transport for 24 hours (best deal for a fleeting visit); an 8-day card (*8-Tage-Umwelt-Streifennetzkarte*) which has 8 units on it, each unit valid for one calendar day, for one person, for

The Jugendstil Karlsplatz Station

unlimited travelling in 'Zone 100', which is practically the whole of Vienna (start inserting with no 1).

For those staying longer it is worth acquiring a *Zeitkarte,* to which must be affixed a passport photo. Tickets of pre-paid unlimited travel for a calendar week, month or year can be purchased at *Tabaks* and stuck on the card.

Uno-City – designed by Johann Staber

PUBLIC TRANSPORT

Buses operating in the Inner City are
marked 'A', those outside it 'B'. Hopper
buses criss-cross the Inner City stopping
at strategic points (Schottentor,
Stephansdom, Graben, Michaelerplatz,
Schwedenplatz, Schwarzenbergplatz,
etc). Eight night buses (N) depart from
Schwedenplatz for the different suburbs.
They run every half hour between
12.30am and 4am. Season tickets are
not valid on them, each journey being
charged at 25 Schillings.

Trams run along the Ringstrasse in both
directions, and on 33 routes out to
virtually all the suburbs.

They run from 5–5.30am to 11pm–
midnight.

Subway trains criss-cross the city centre
– there are currently five lines and the
service is improving all the time. They
run from about 5am to midnight.

Schnellbahn lines dovetail with subway
stations, and primarily serve outlying
districts for commuters. They run from
4.30–5am to 9–midnight.

It is unwise to try and travel on the
system without paying – controls are
regular, and on the spot fines start at 400
Schillings.

Taxis can be found at ranks at all
stations and the airport, as well as at
many strategic places around town
(tel: 40 100).

RADIO

News in English at 8am every morning on the first programme of Austrian Radio (Ö1). Blue Danube Radio (102.2 MHz FM) has English language news at 7am, noon and 6pm.

READING

Of locally published volumes two may be especially recommended:
Richard Rickett -
A Brief Survey of Austrian History
Richard Rickett -
Music and Musicians in Vienna.
Both are published by Prachner. Paul Hofmann's *The Viennese* is a lively, if rather hostile, journey round the Viennese psyche. (Published by Anchor Books.)

SENIOR CITIZENS

Discounts are available for travel in Austria and entrance fees to museums.

STUDENT AND YOUTH TRAVEL

Students with valid student cards can get some fares discounted and reductions on museum entrance fees. **Jugend – info Wien** (Dr-Karl-Renner-Ring/Bellaria Passage, tel: 526 46 37) is open Monday to Friday, noon– 7pm and Saturdays

Traditional street entertainment

10am– 7pm. It can assist with information about cheap accommodation, cheap eating, and tickets for events at reduced prices, which can also be bought here. Tourist Information Offices also have copies of *Youth Scene Vienna*, a magazine packed with useful tips.

There are nine youth hostels in Vienna, six of them open all the year round, the others from spring or summer to autumn.

TELEPHONES

Telephone booths are scattered all over Vienna and have panels which include instructions in English. Not all of them are equipped for long-distance calls but it will be clear from the instructions if they are. Telephone cards *(Telefon- wertkarten)* can be purchased in post offices or in *Trafiks* in sums of 50 and 100 Schillings. The magnetic strip debits the cost of the call from the card. On the corner of Wallnerstrasse (off Kohlmarkt) and Goldschmiedgasse (near Stephansplatz) is a telephone that accepts credit cards. You may also phone from post offices (book your line at the counter, pay at the end). It is cheaper to phone at weekends and after 6pm, or before 8am.

Country codes are as follows, (prefaced by 00):

Australia	0061
Canada	001
Ireland	00353
New Zealand	0064
UK	0044
US	001

Information: (Austria) 1611; (direct dial abroad) 08; (operator for foreign calls) 09.

For individual cities see the first pages of the phone book (first volume).

TIME
Vienna is on Central European Time: 4 1/2–10 hours ahead of Canada; 7–9 hours later than Australia; 11 hours later than New Zealand; one hour ahead of GMT (two hours in summer); six hours ahead of New York.

TIPPING
10–15 per cent for the usual services.

TOILETS
Restaurants and museums all have them. There are clean and rather aesthetic Jugendstil WCs on the Graben. *Damen* (Ladies), *Herren* (Gentlemen).

TOURIST INFORMATION
At Schwechat Airport (open: 8.30am–10pm, until 11pm from June to September))
Kärntner Strasse 38 *(open: 9am–7pm, tel: 513 88 92)*
Wien Auhof *(for motorists approaching from the West Motorway, open: 8am–10pm, 10am–6pm in winter)*
Wien Zentrum *(for motorists approaching from Southern Motorway, open: 8am–10pm, 10am–6pm in winter)*

The Austrian National Tourist Board is represented abroad as follows:
Australia *19th Floor, 1 York Street,*

Scene from the opera Turandot

Sydney 2000 NSW (tel: 241 1916).
Canada *2 Bloor Street East, Suite 3330, Toronto, Ontario (tel: 967 3381).*
New Zealand *76 Symonds Street, Seventh Floor, PO Box 310, Auckland (tel: 734 078).*
UK *30 St George Street, London WIR OAL (tel: (071) 629 0461).*
US *500 Fifth Avenue, New York, NY 10110 (tel: (212) 944 6880);*
11601 Wilshire Boulevard, Los Angeles Ca 90025 (tel: (213) 477 3332);
500 North Michigan Avenue, Chicago Ill 60611 (tel: (312) 644 5556);
1300 Post Oak Boulevard, Houston Tx 77056 (tel: (713) 850 9999).
Thomas Cook is located at Reisen & Freizeit, Mariahilferstrasse 20.

VIENNA THROUGH THE YEAR
January/February: Carnival.
The Ball Season.
March: Haydn Festival.
Vienna Film Festival.
April: Spring Festival in the Prater.
May/June: Festival of Vienna (Arts/Music)
July/August: Music Festival.
September: Opera Season begins.
Trade Fair.
November: Schubert festival.
Antiques Fair.
December: Advent Markets throughout the city.

ACKNOWLEDGEMENTS

The Automobile Association wishes to thank the following photographers and libraries and the Austrian National Tourist Office for their assistance in the preparation of this book.

MARTYN ADELMAN p9 Tourists, tourist buses, p90/1 Liechtenstein Palace
AUSTRIAN NATIONAL TOURIST OFFICE p4 Ringstrasse, p9 Karl-Marx-Hof, p10 Opera, p12 rooftop view, p13 River Danube, p14 village, p18 Café Central, p20 Vienna rooftops, p47 café, p49 stairway, p67 statue, crown, p72/3 Spanish Riding School, p80 carriage door, p91 Obizzi Palais, p92 Palais-Kinsky, p98 Prater swings, p101 Ringstrasse, p105 Schönbrunn salon, p106 theatre, p108 Goethe monument, p114 Kaisergruft, p119 Wotrubakirche, p121 Kursalon, p122 Volksgarten, p123 cemetery, graves, p125 vineyards, tavern, p128 UNO City, p129 Wienerwald, p131 Jugendstil, p134 Durnstein, p135 Melk, p138 moat, p139 windsurfers, p147 theatre, p152 Staatsoper, p153 Vienna Boys' Choir, p157 Clown Museum, p159 horseriding, p160 food, p161 Stelzenessen restaurant, p166 enjoying coffee, p171 entertainers, p190 Opera.
MARY EVANS PICTURE LIBRARY p89 elegance of the waltz
MUSEUM DER STADTWEIN p7 circular plan, p64 painting, p65 armour
MUSEUM MODERNER p78
ZEFA PICTURE LIBRARY p17 Vienna National Theatre, p18 State Opera House, p75 sculpture, p183 view, p188 UNO City
All the remaining photographs are in The Automobile Association's picture library with contributions from David Noble and Michael Siebert.